THANK YOU FOR YOUR PURCHASE OF

DINOSAUR LIFE

COLORING BOOK FOR ALL AGES

BY KRISTY SPECHT

ISBN-13: 978-0692085417
ISBN-10: 0692085416

Facebook Page @ https://www.facebook.com/TheeComicalArtist

Follow me on Instagram @theecomicalartist

This book is self-published.

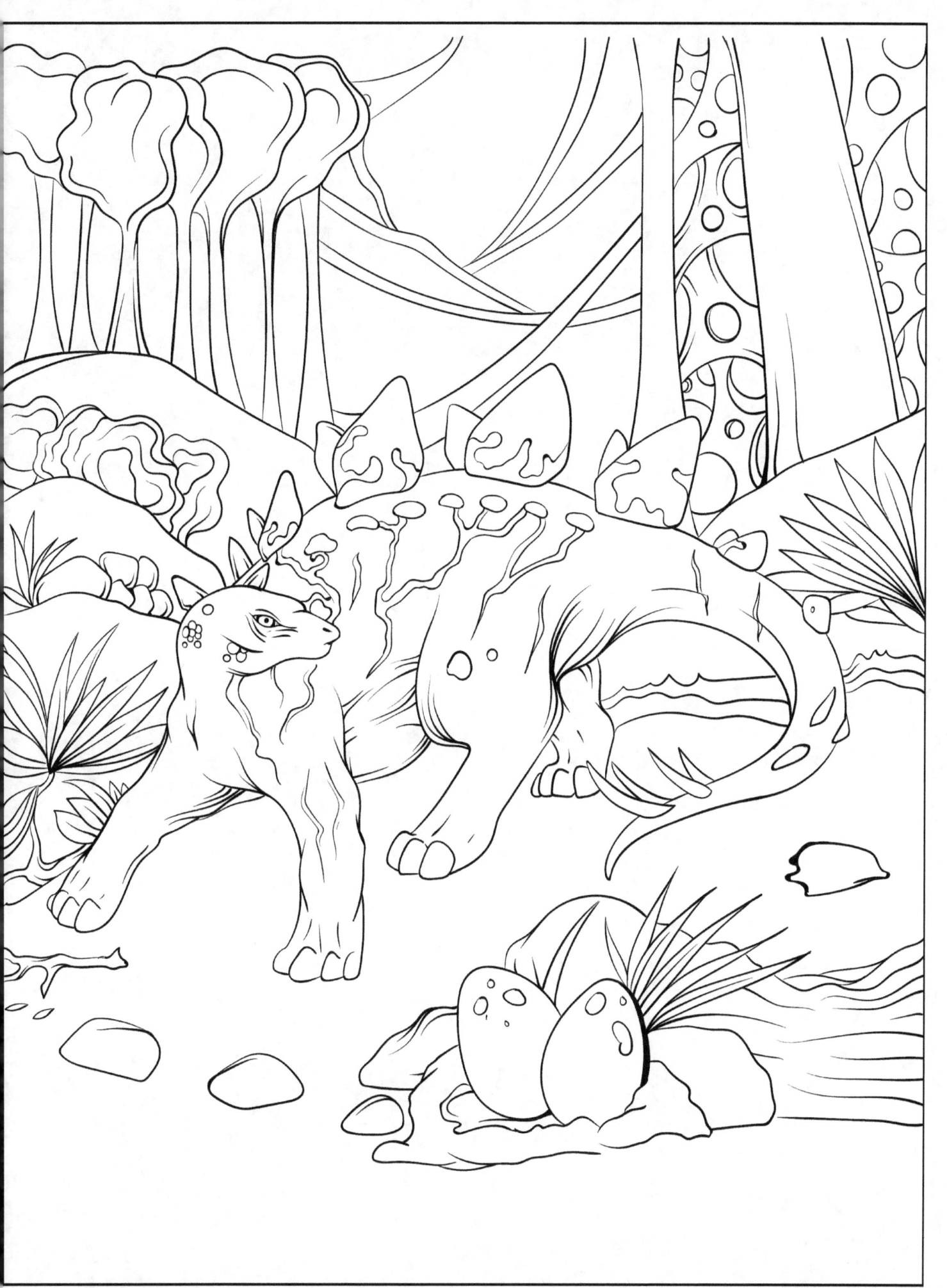

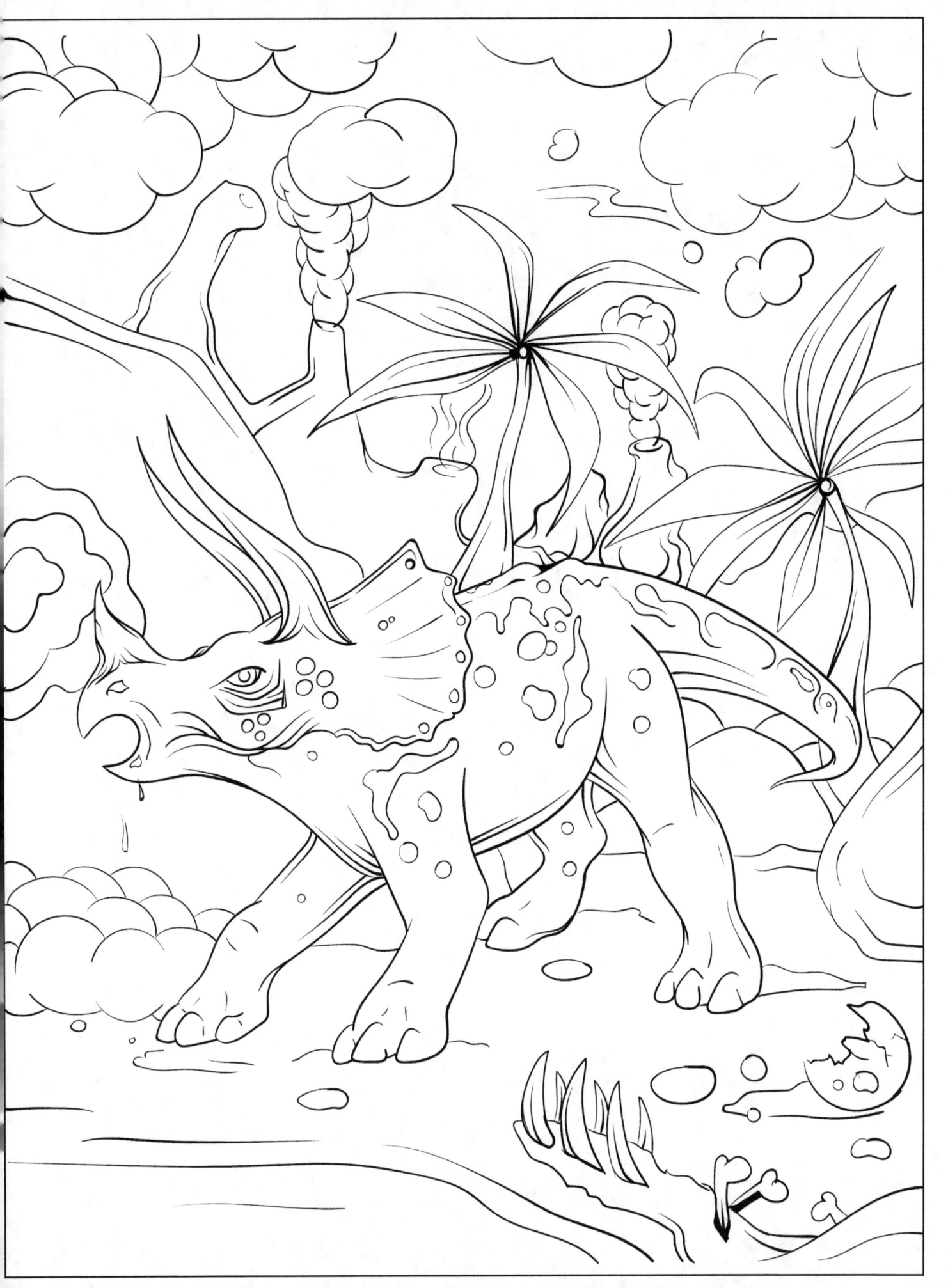

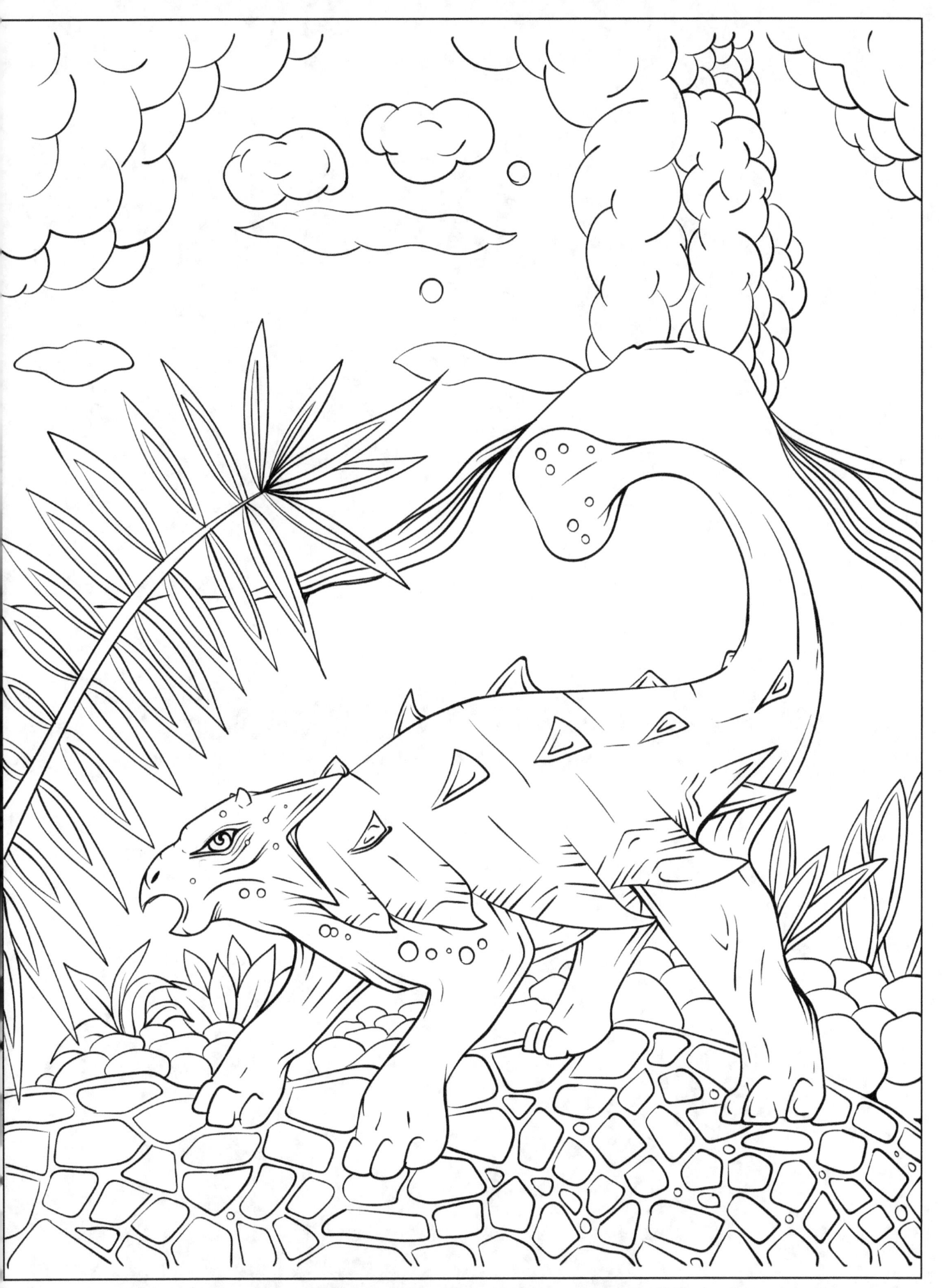

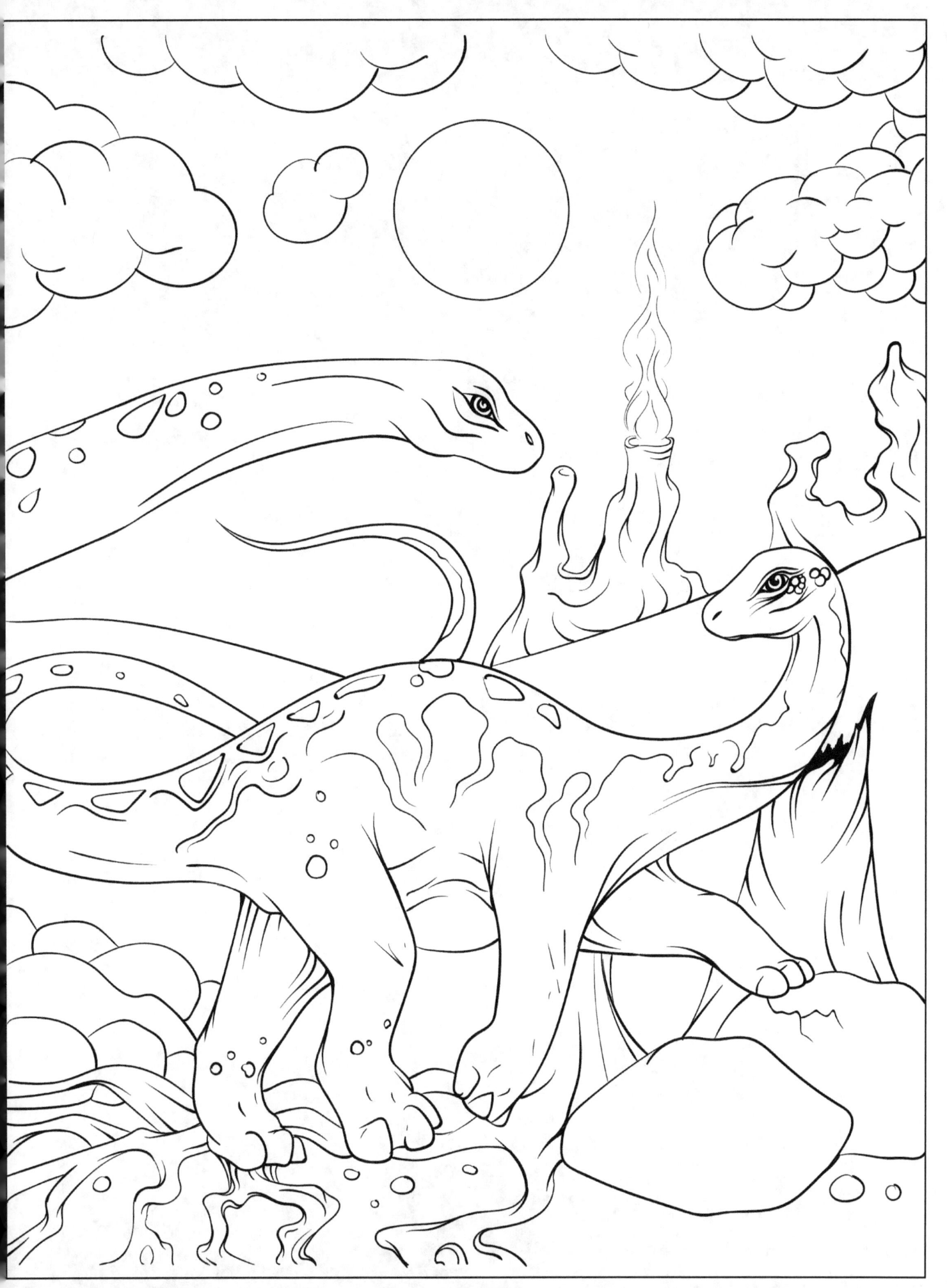

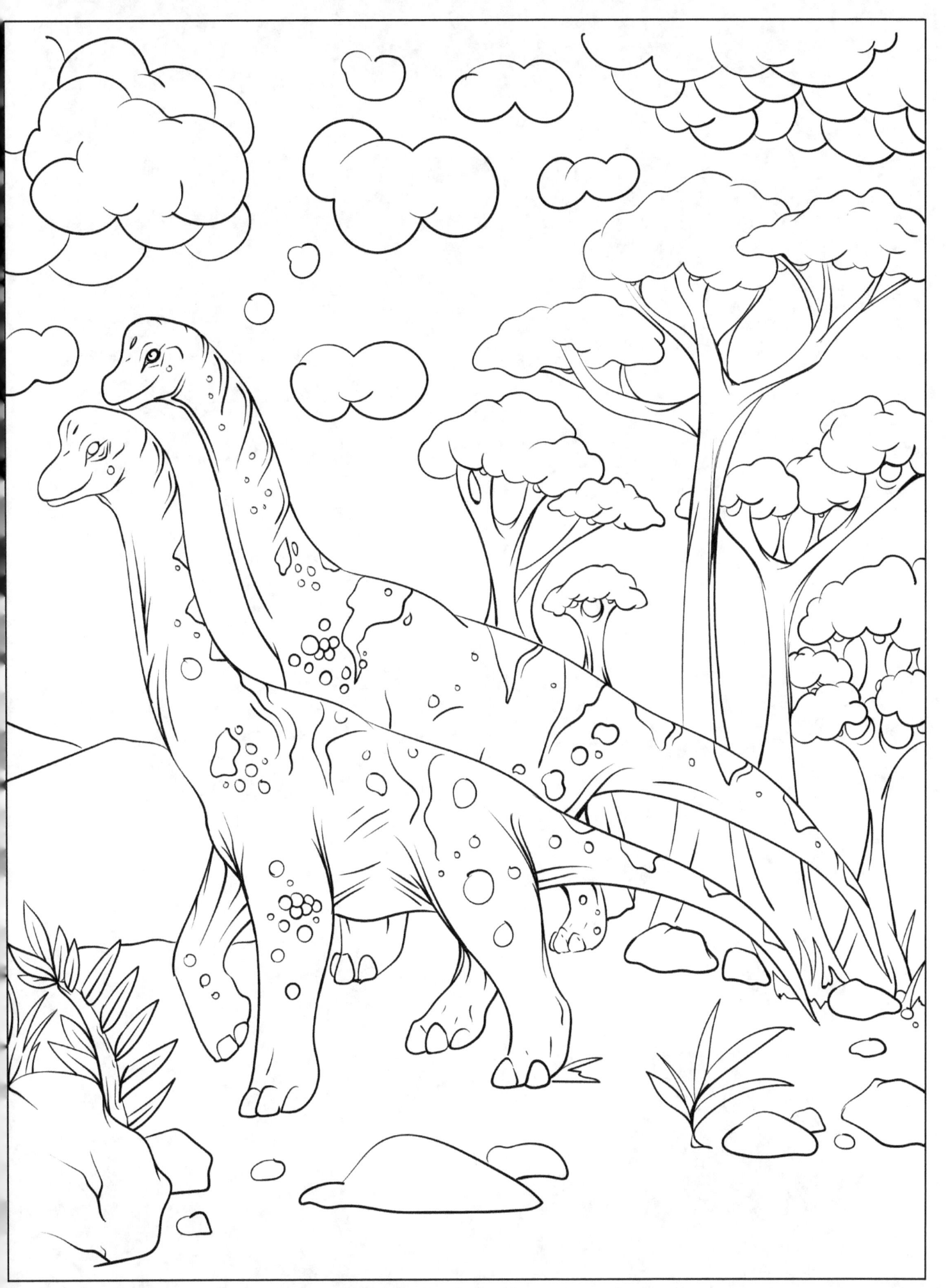

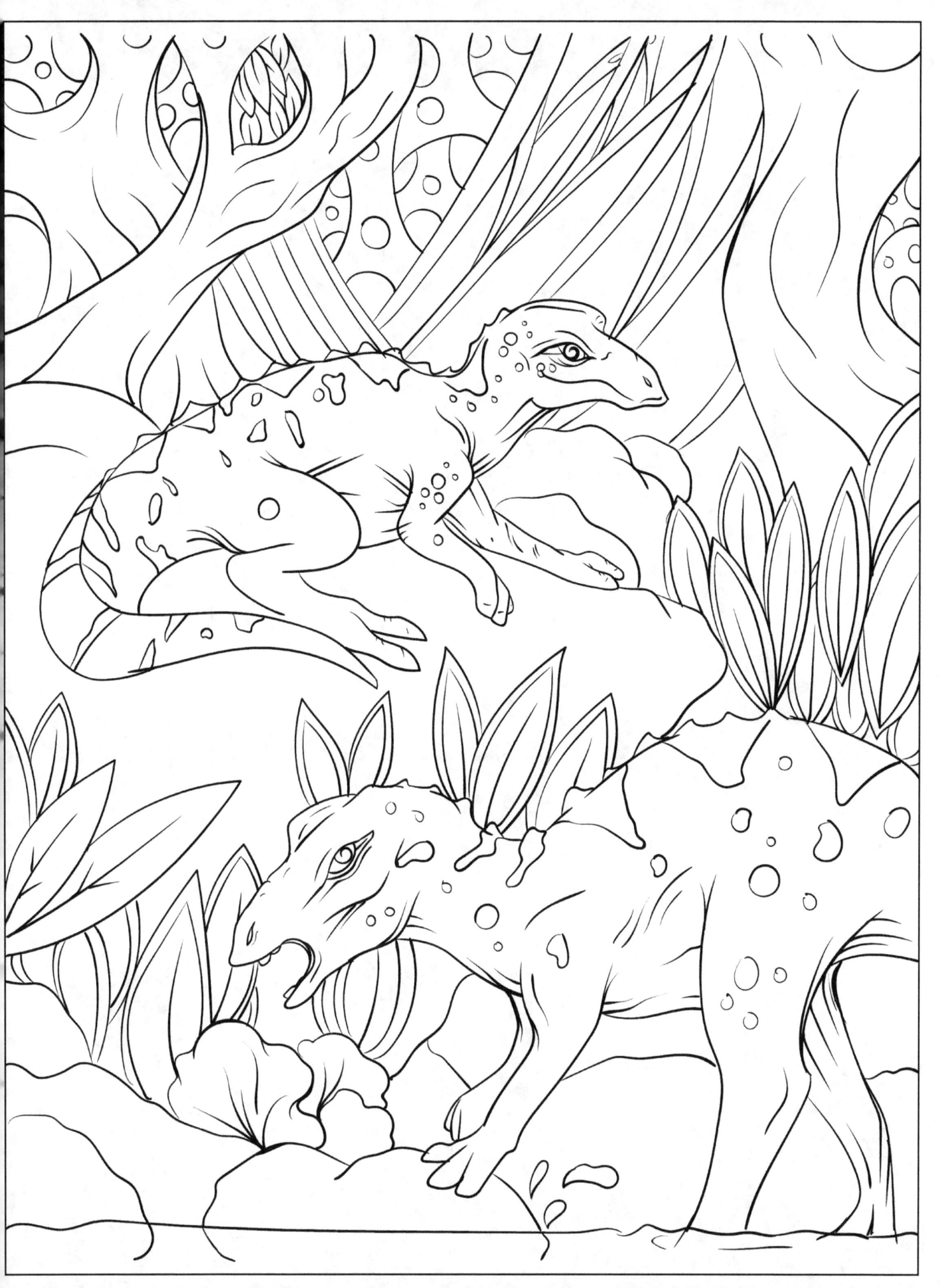

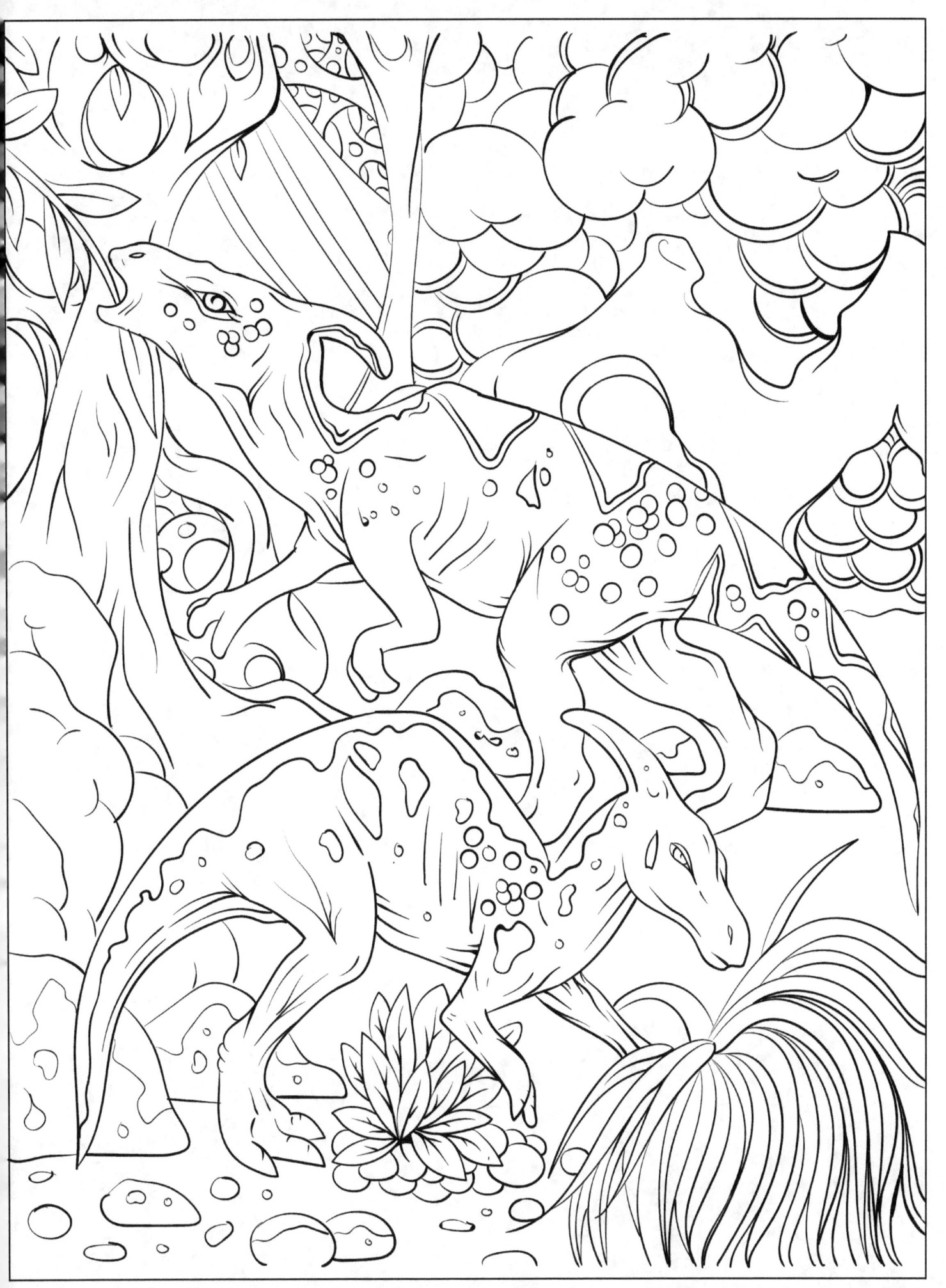

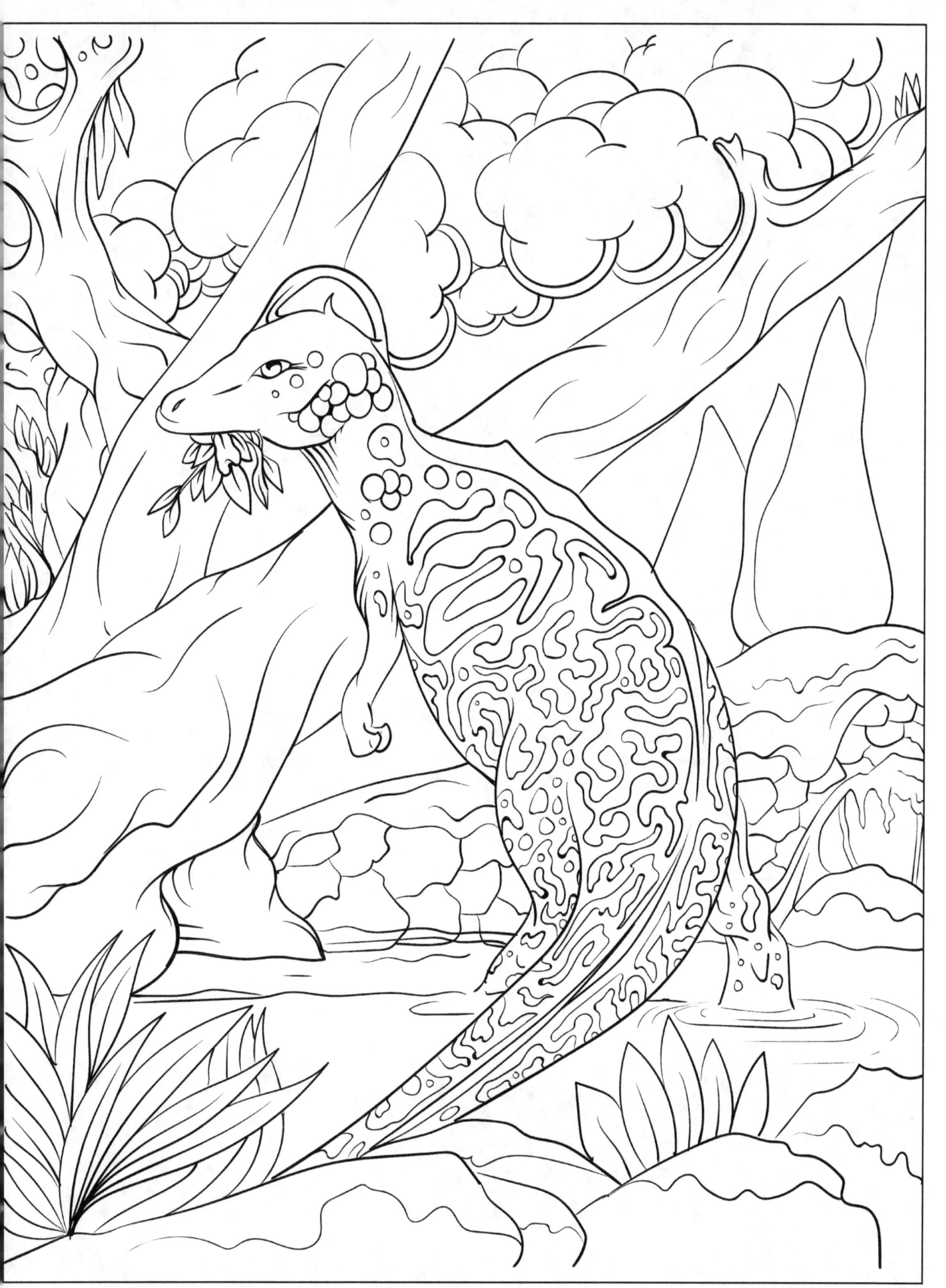

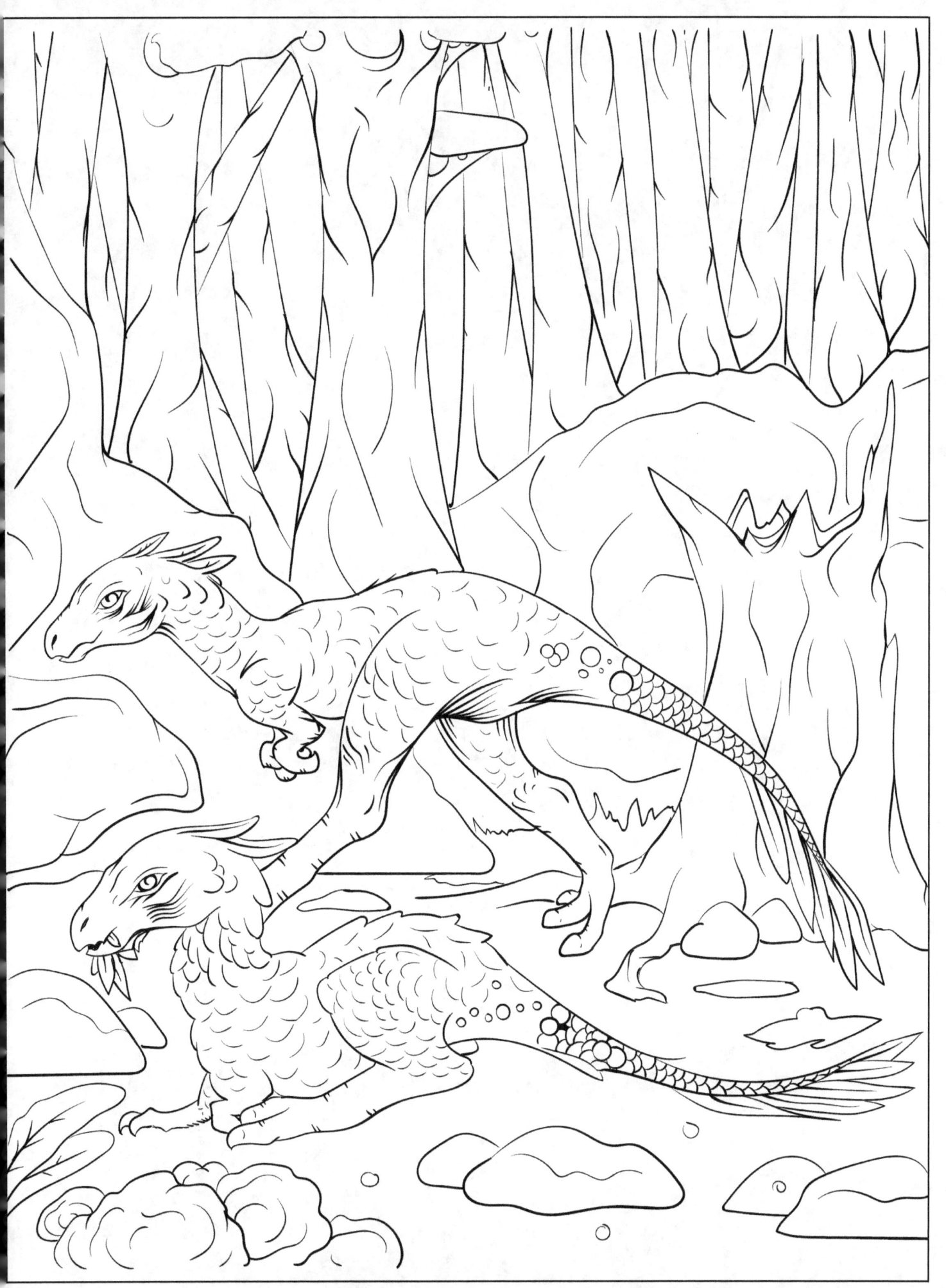

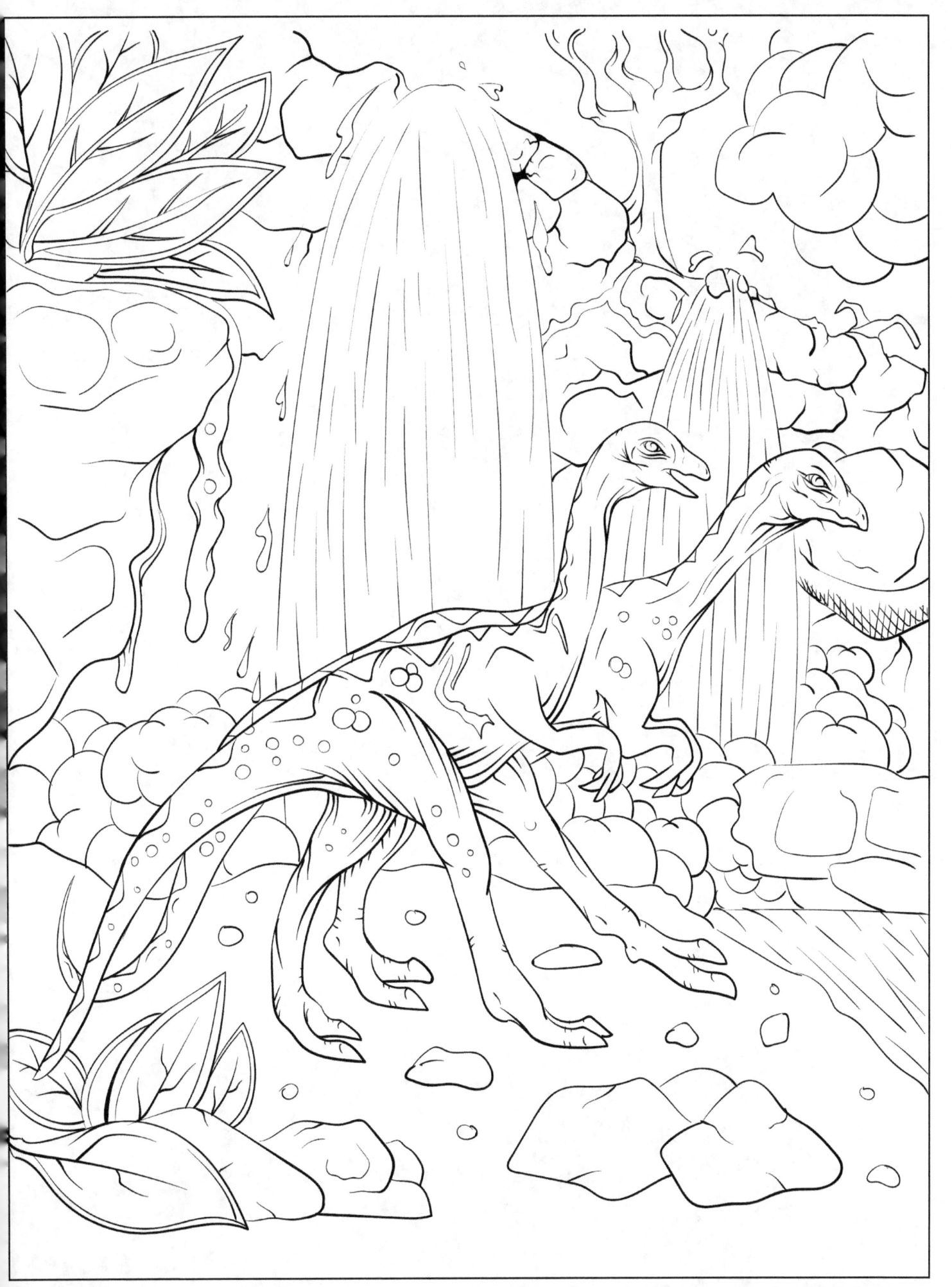

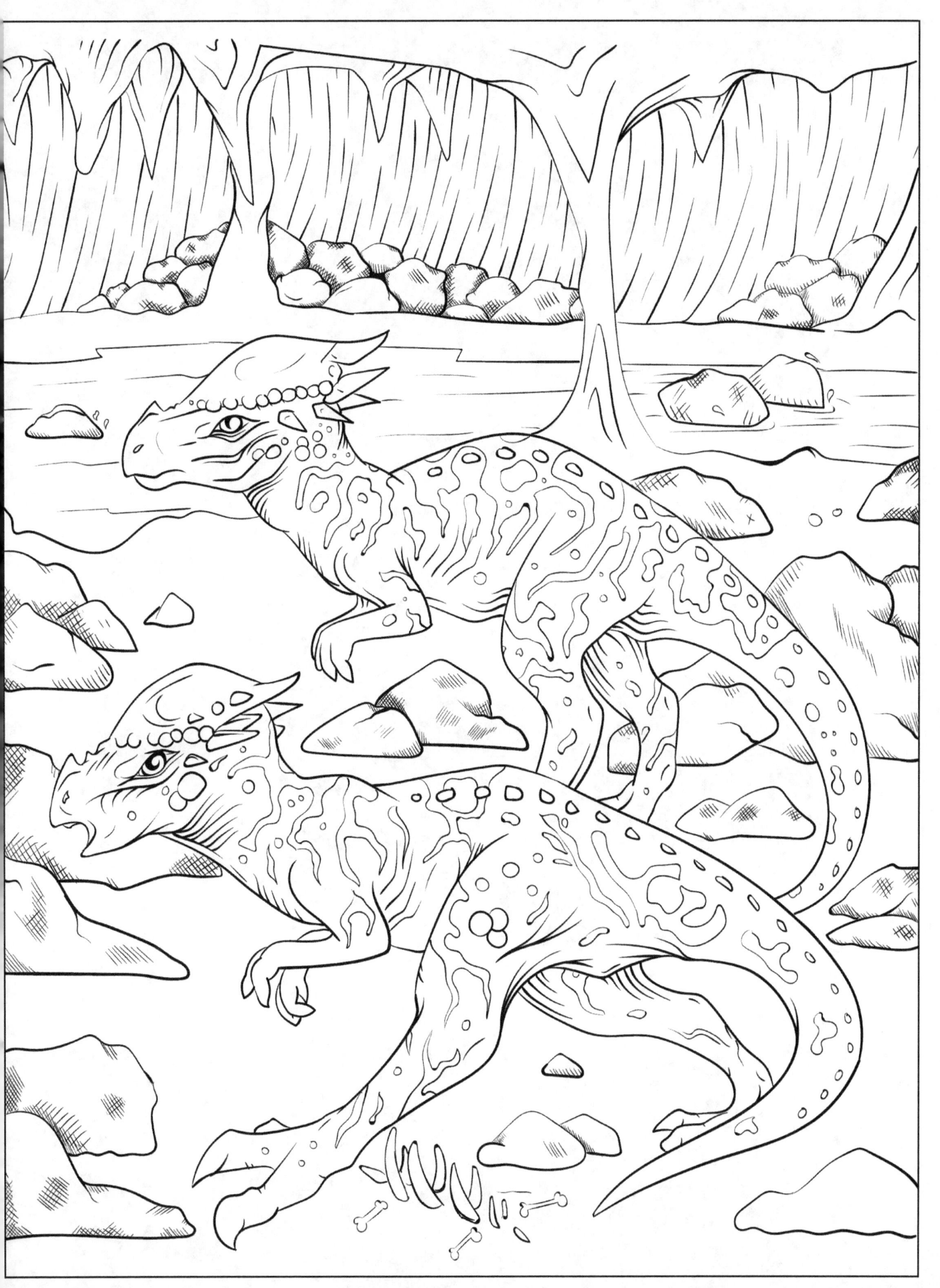

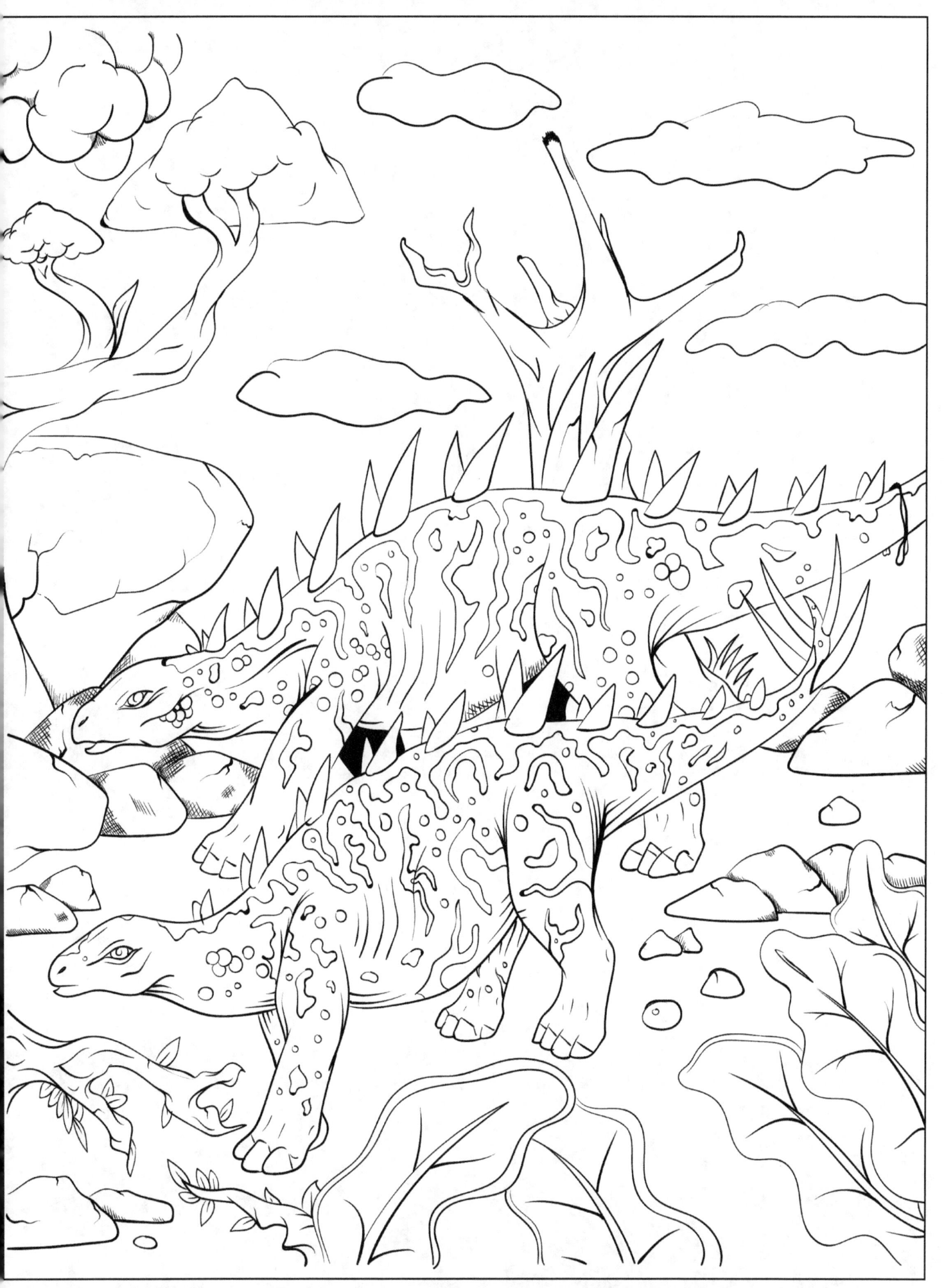

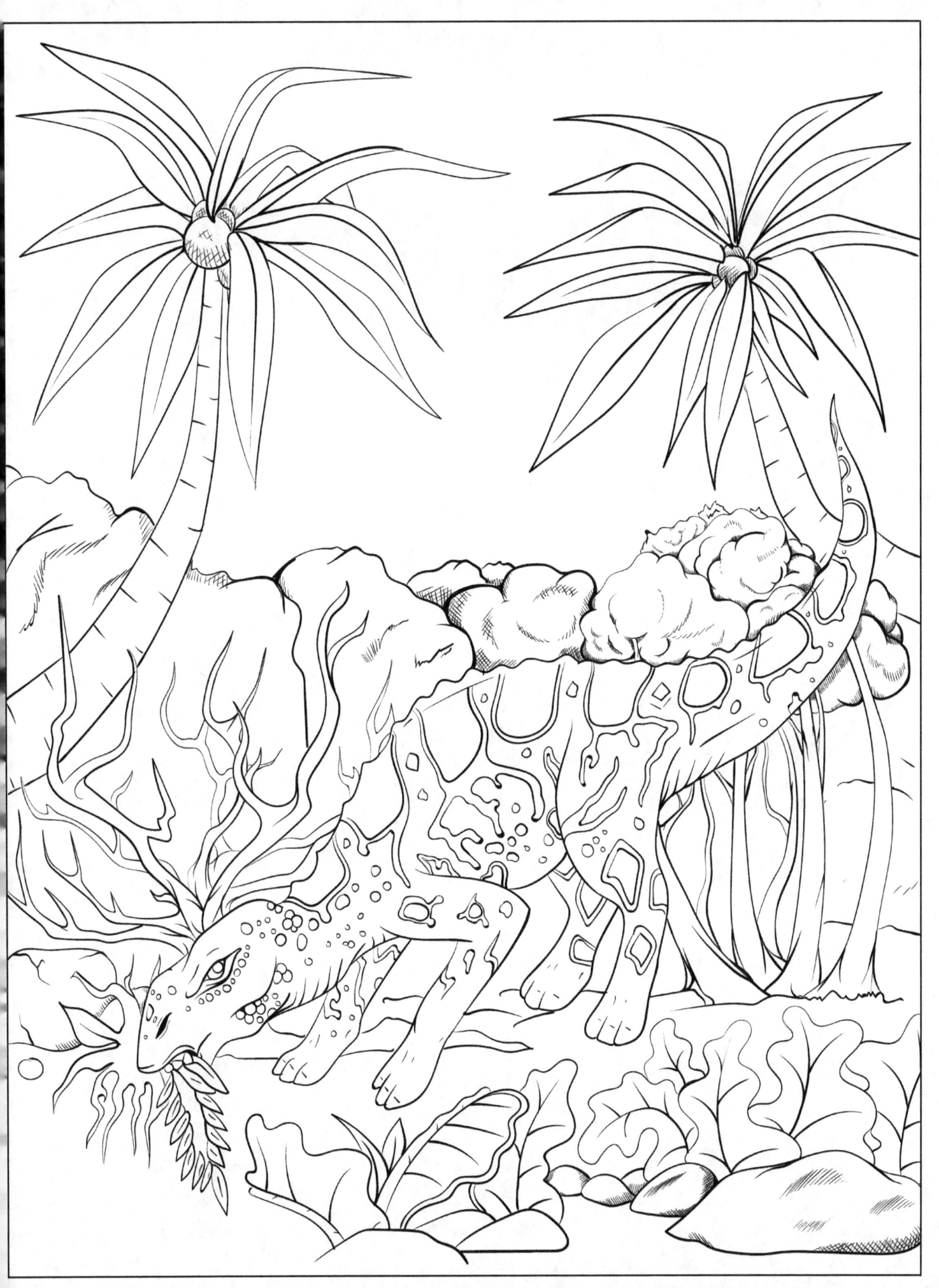

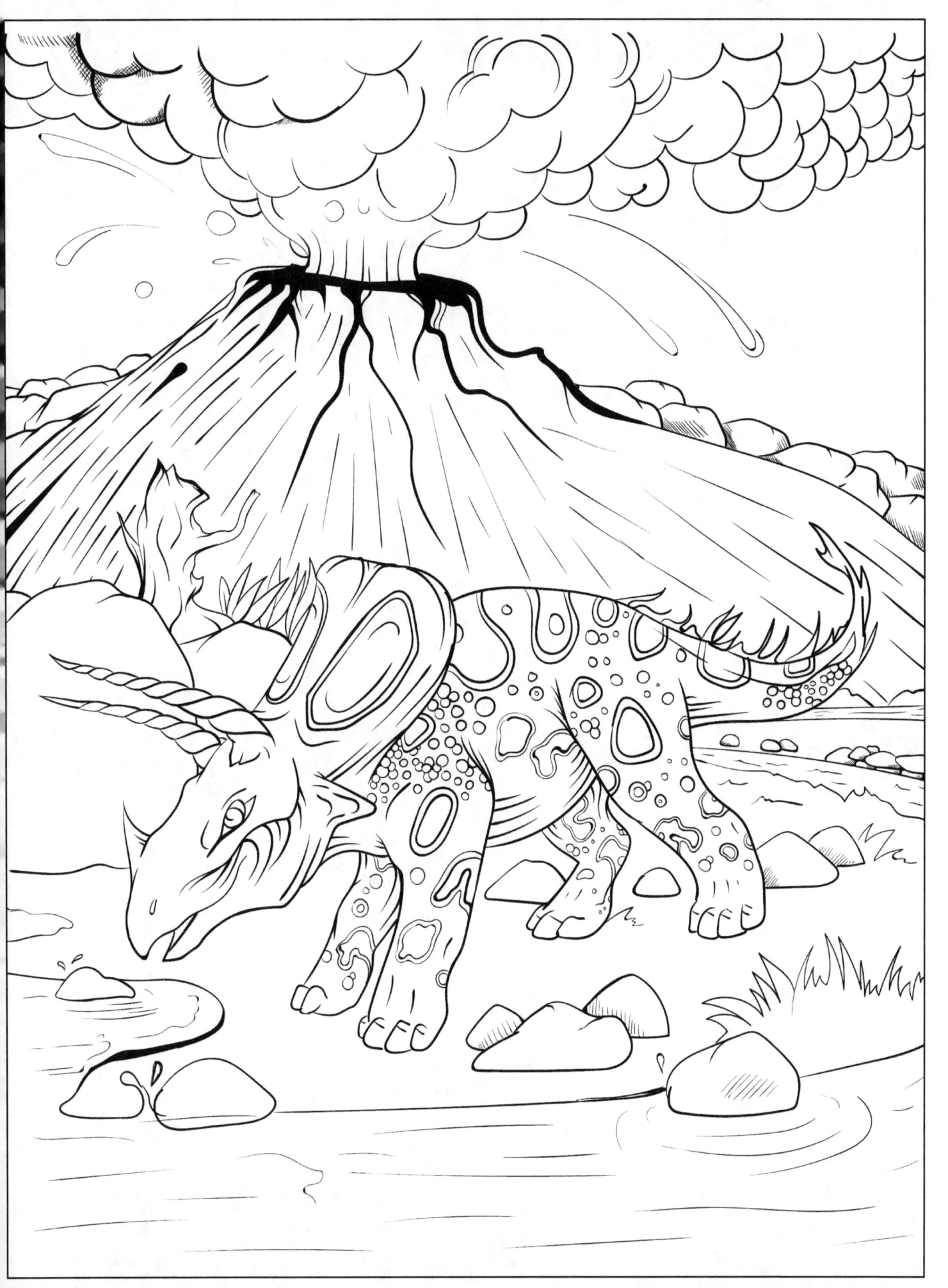

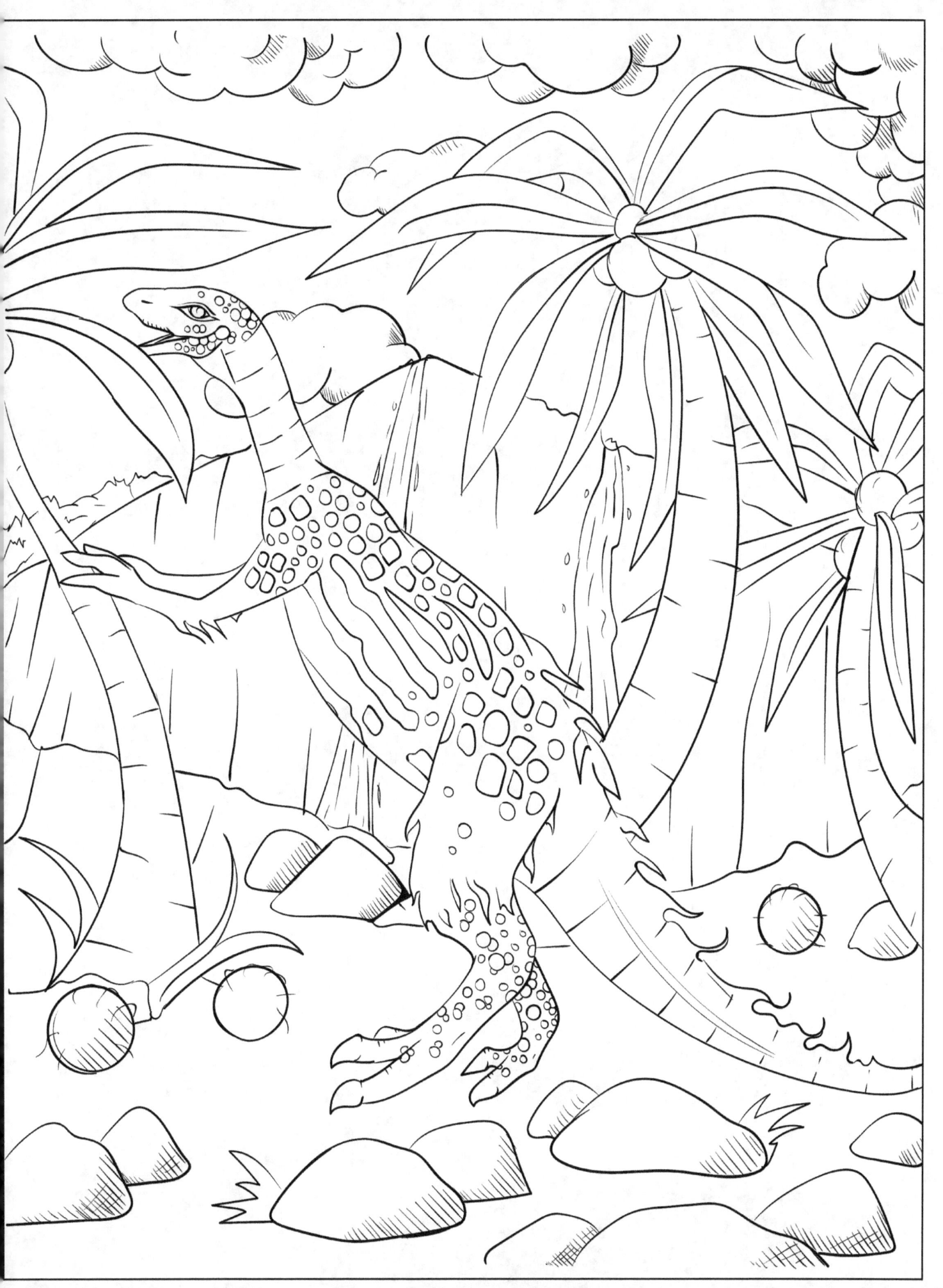

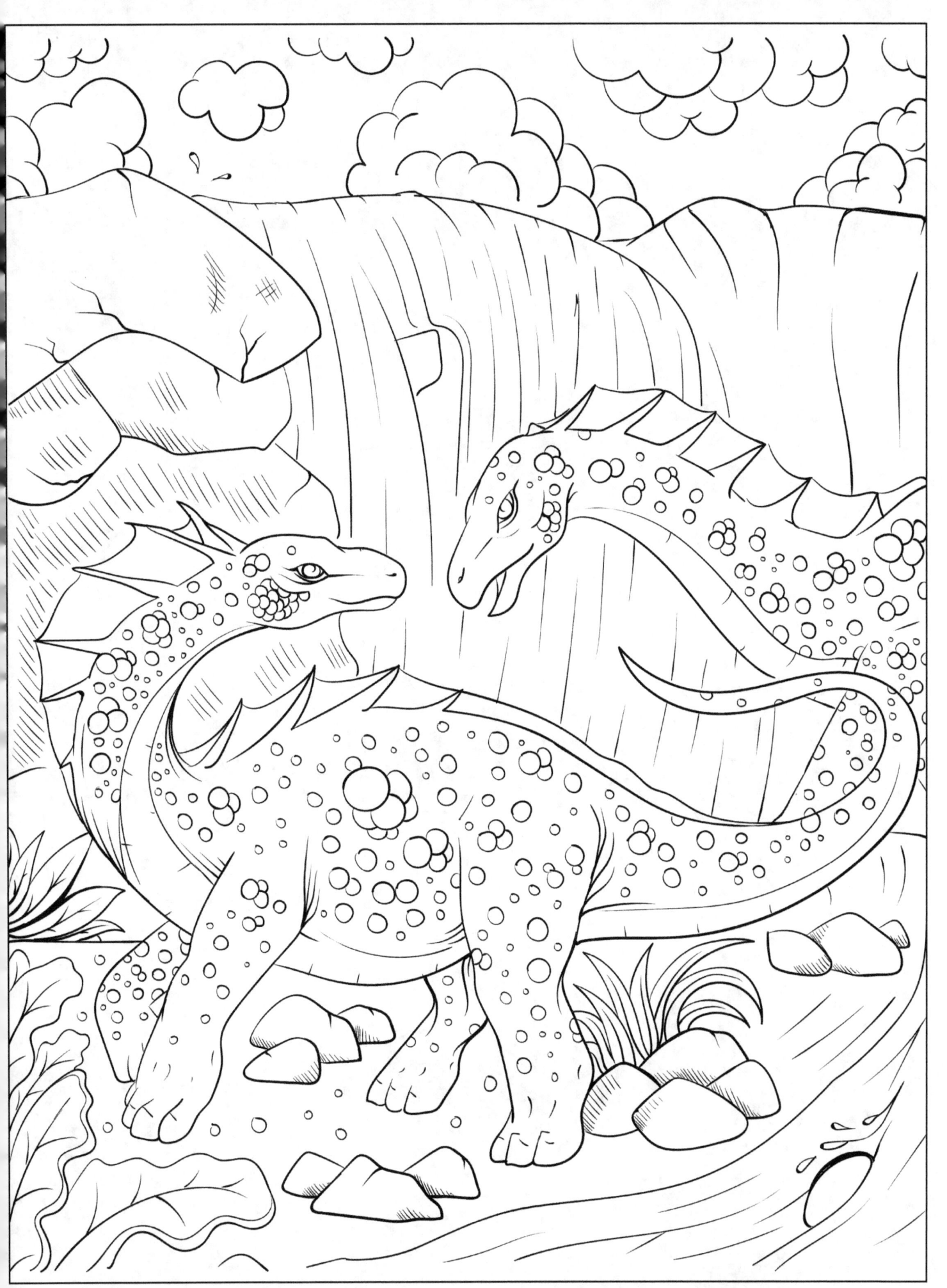

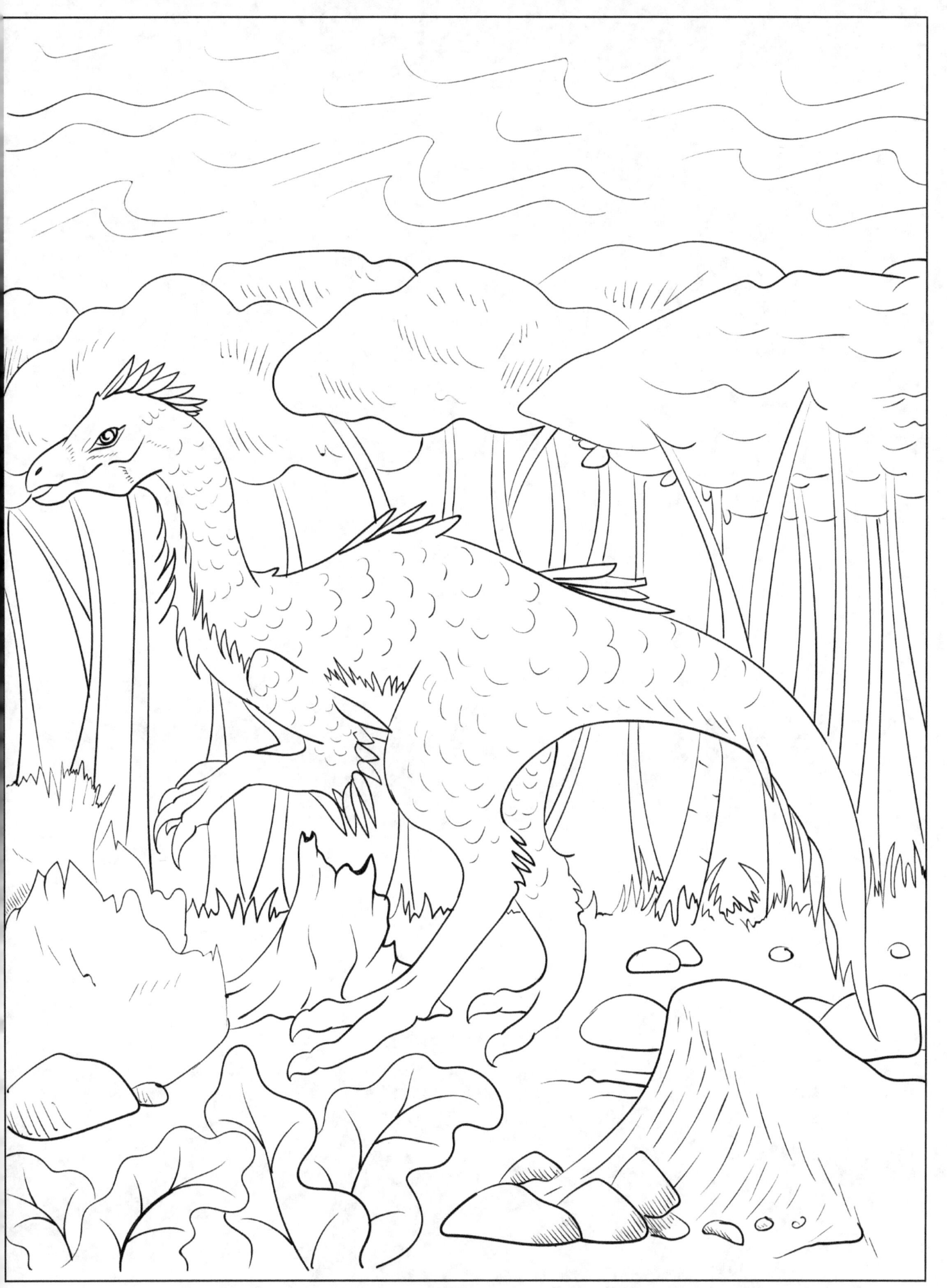

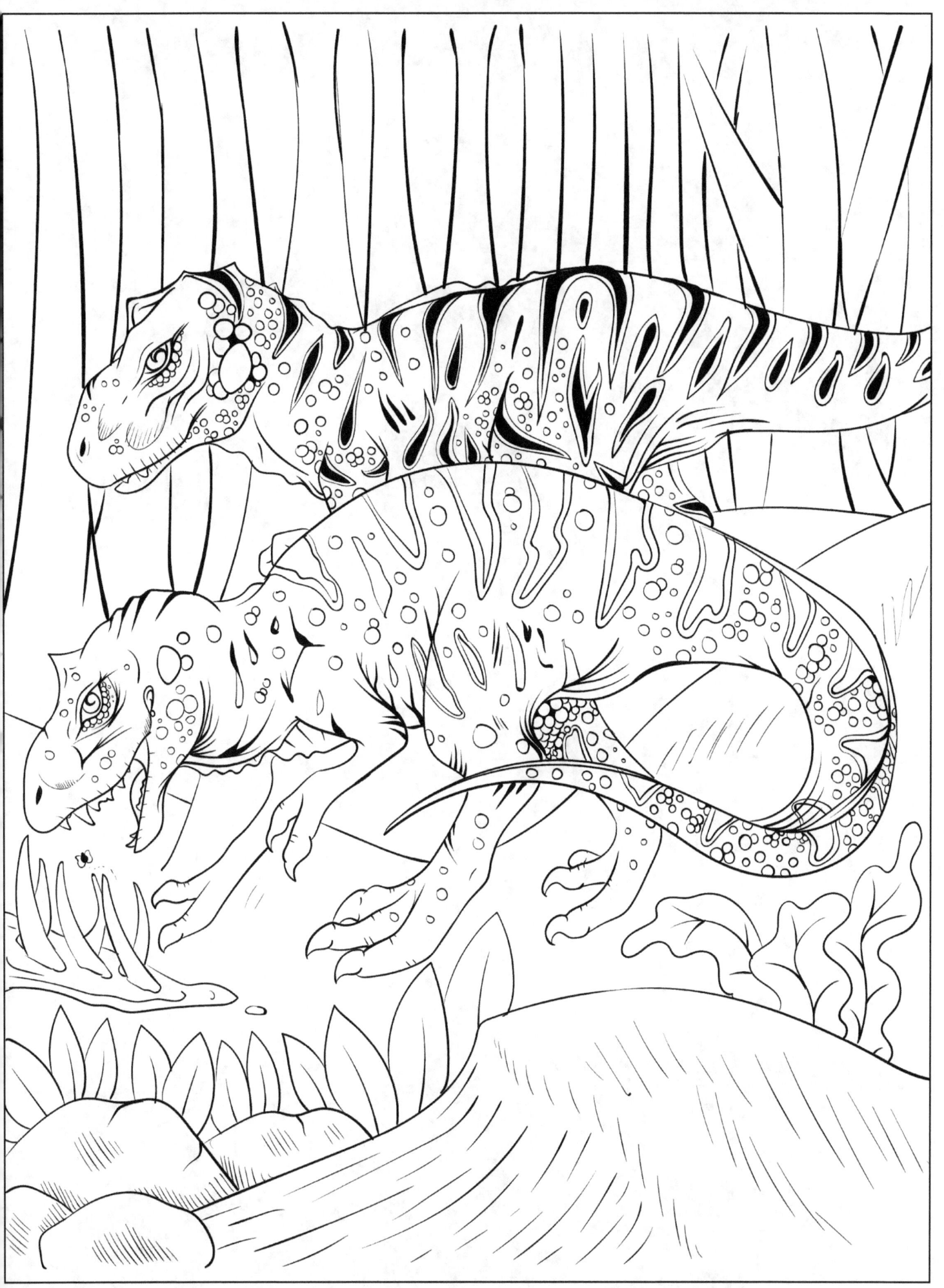

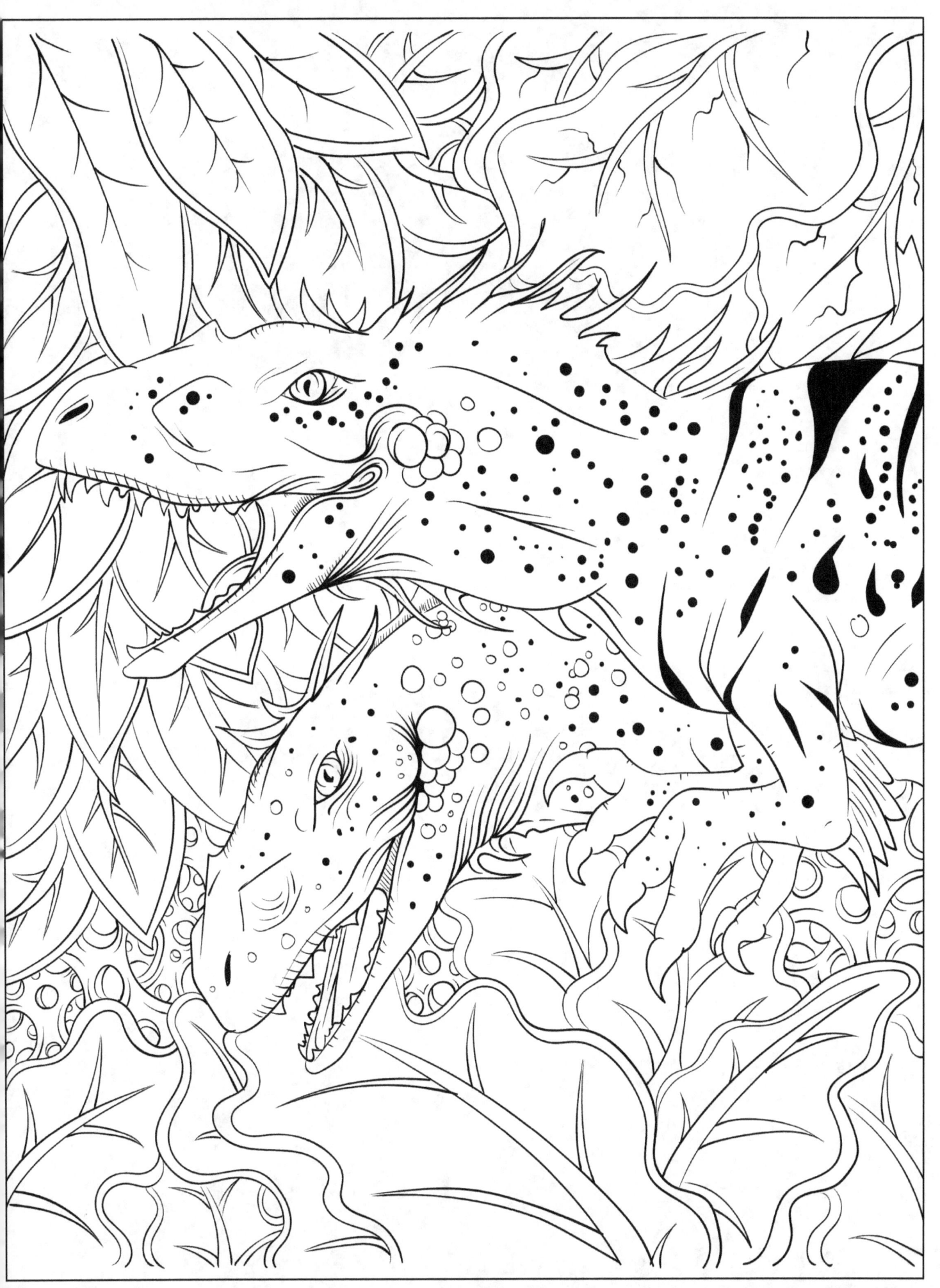

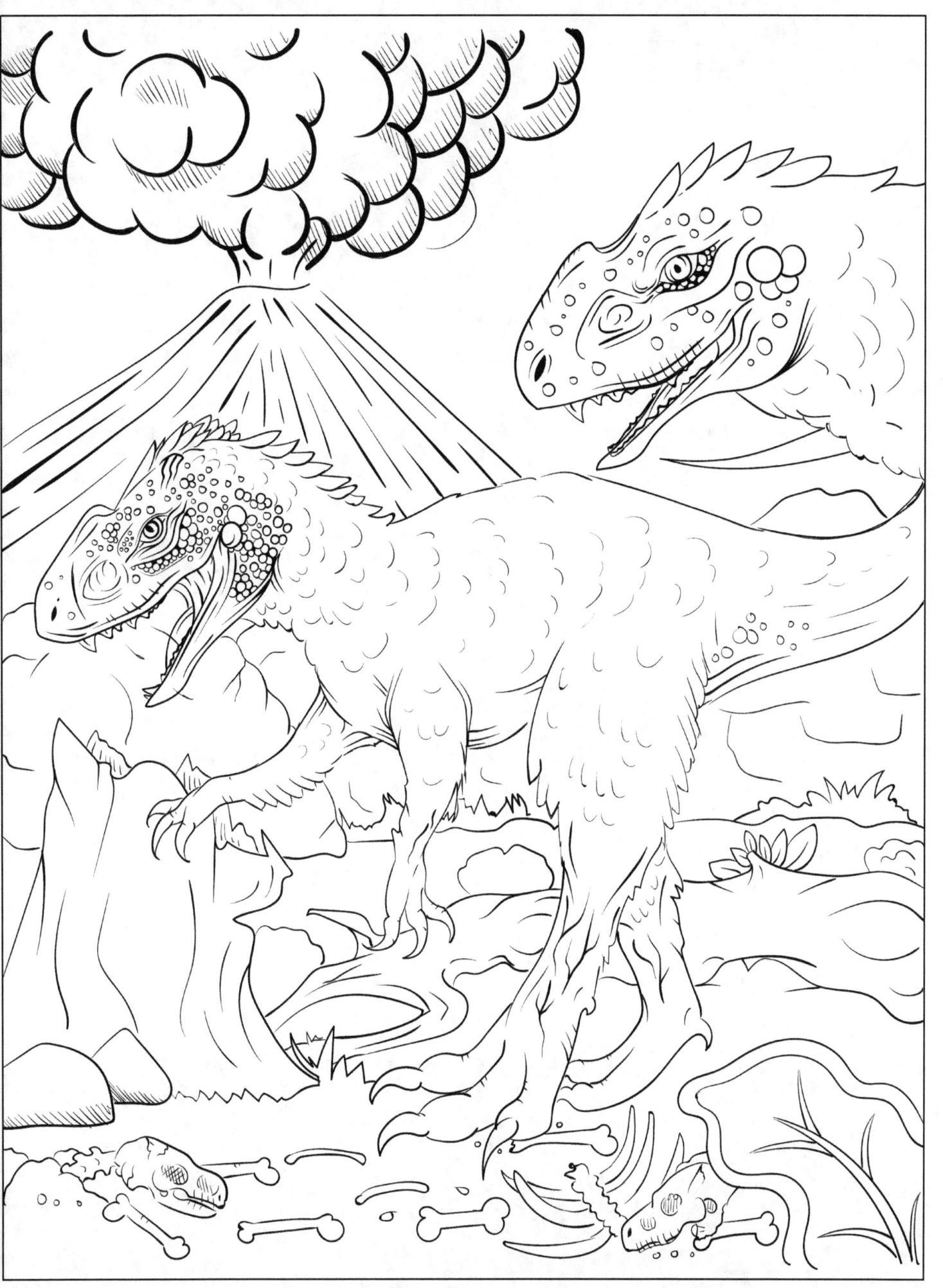

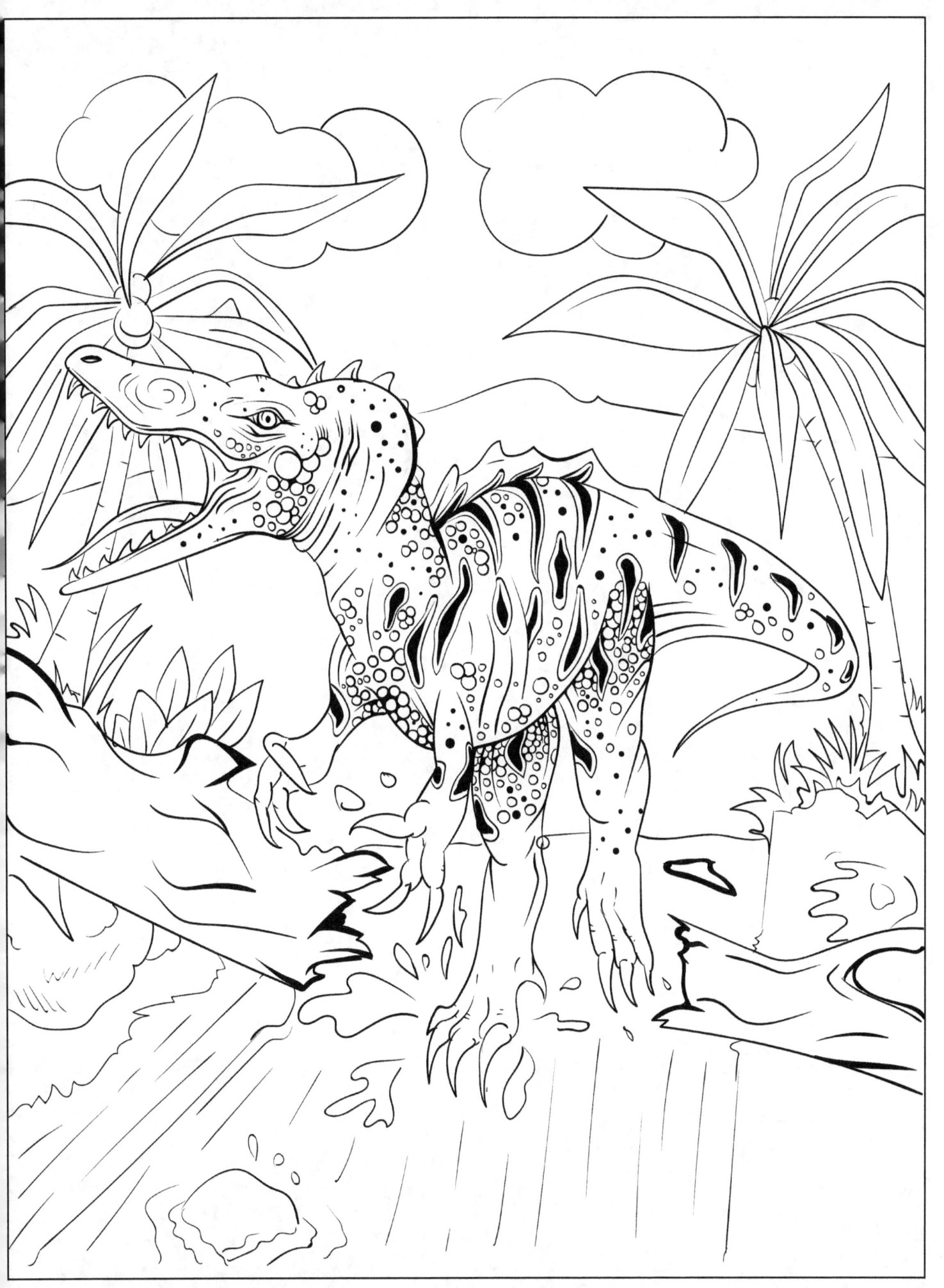

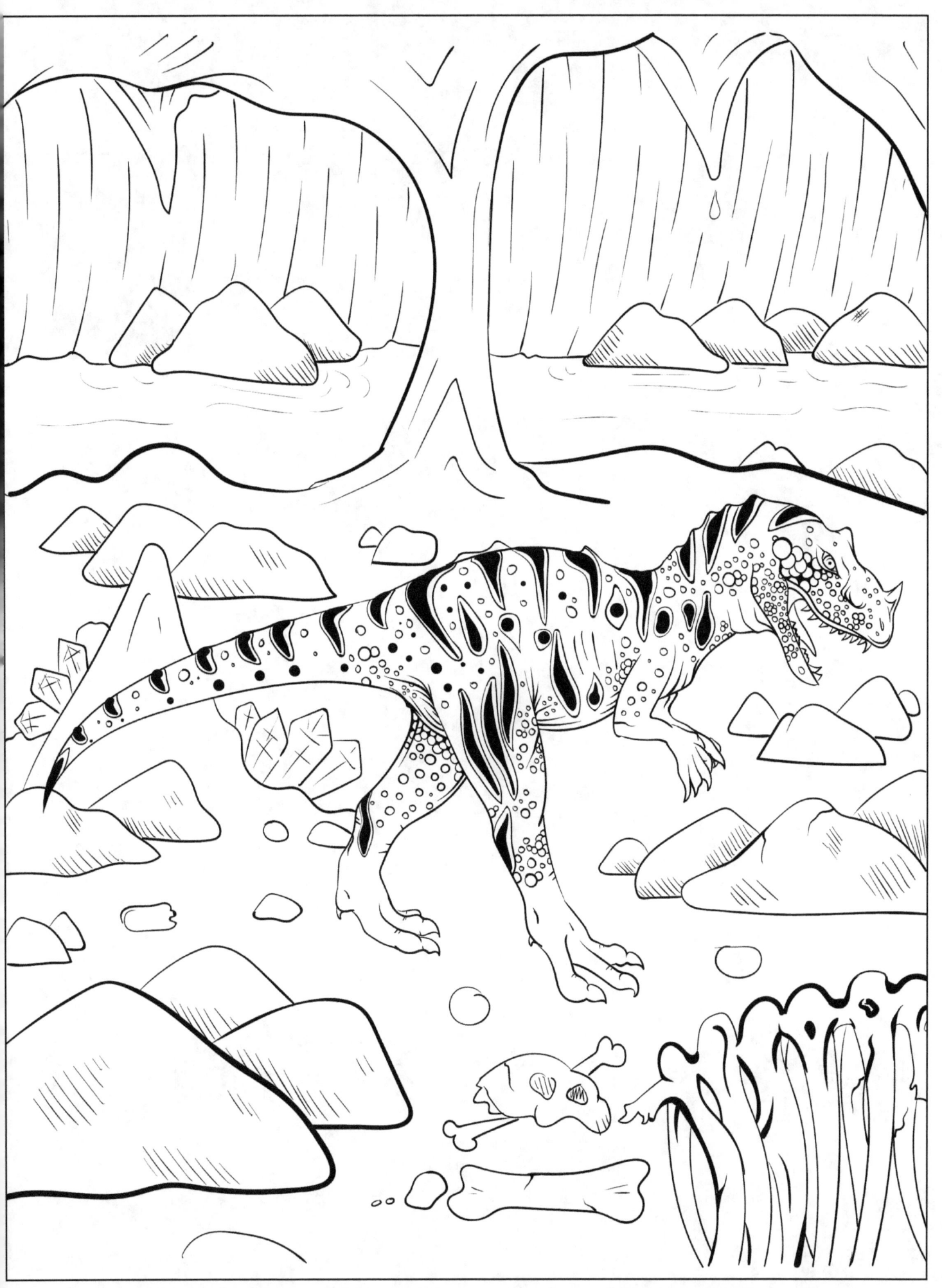

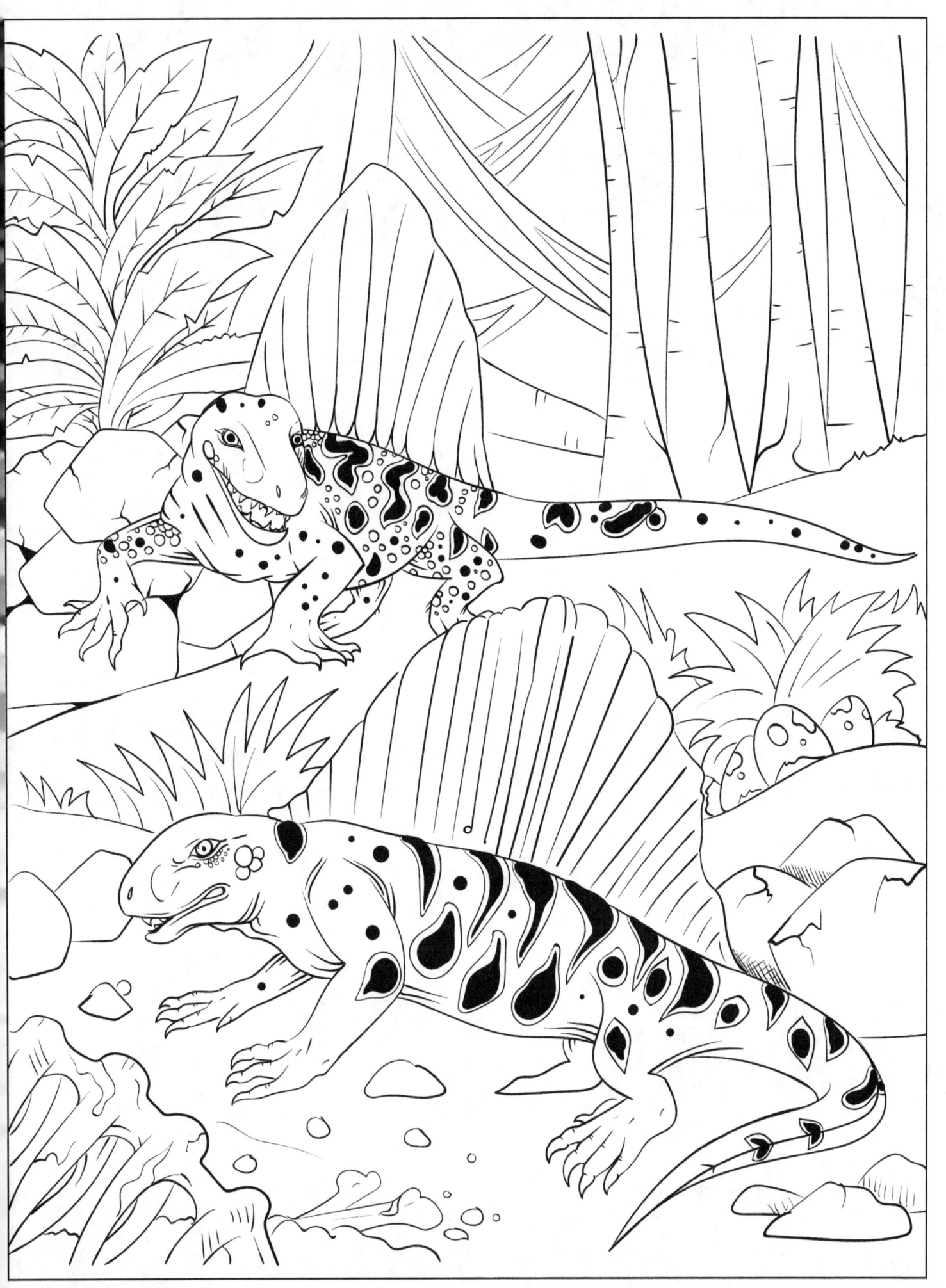

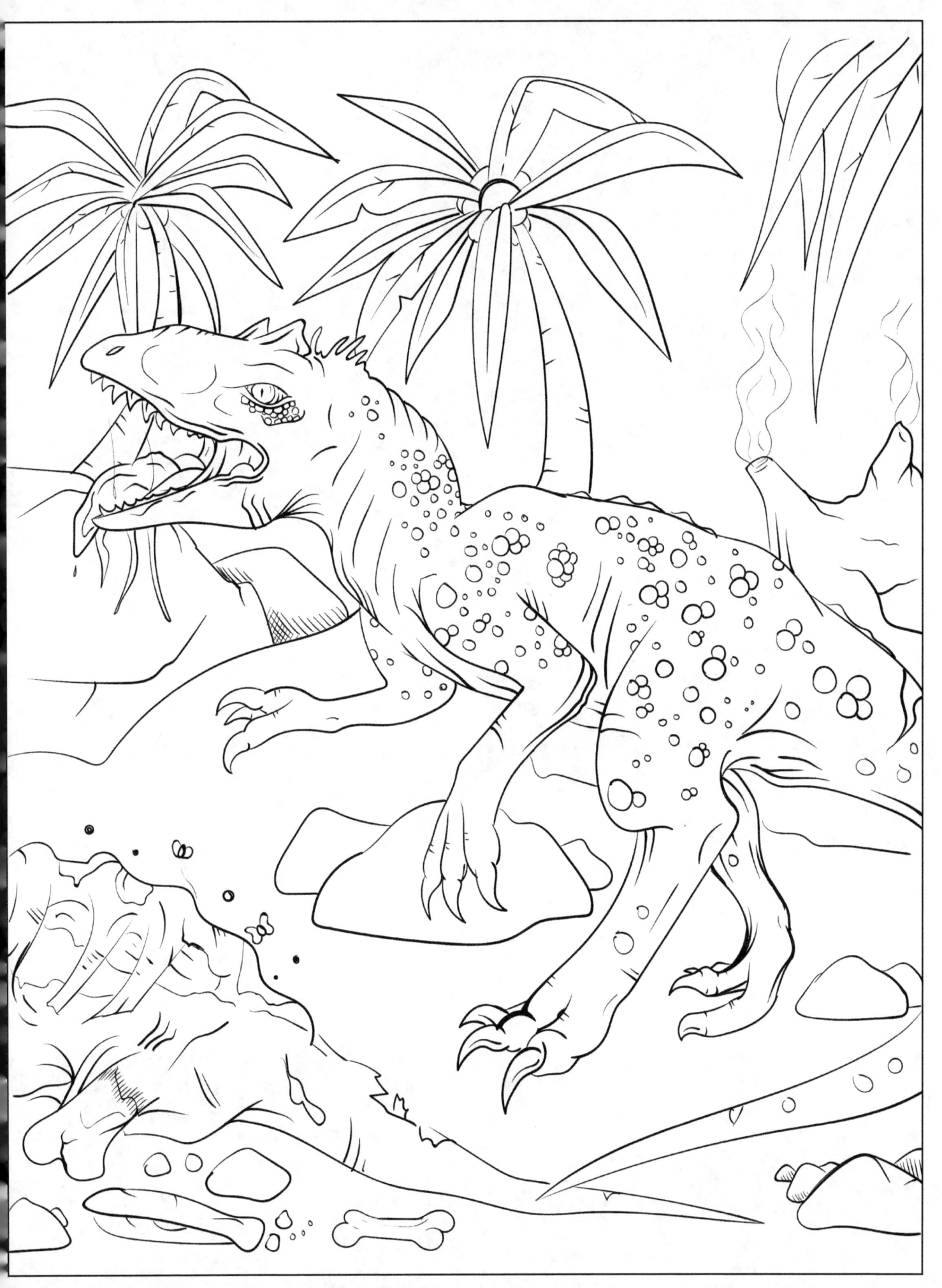

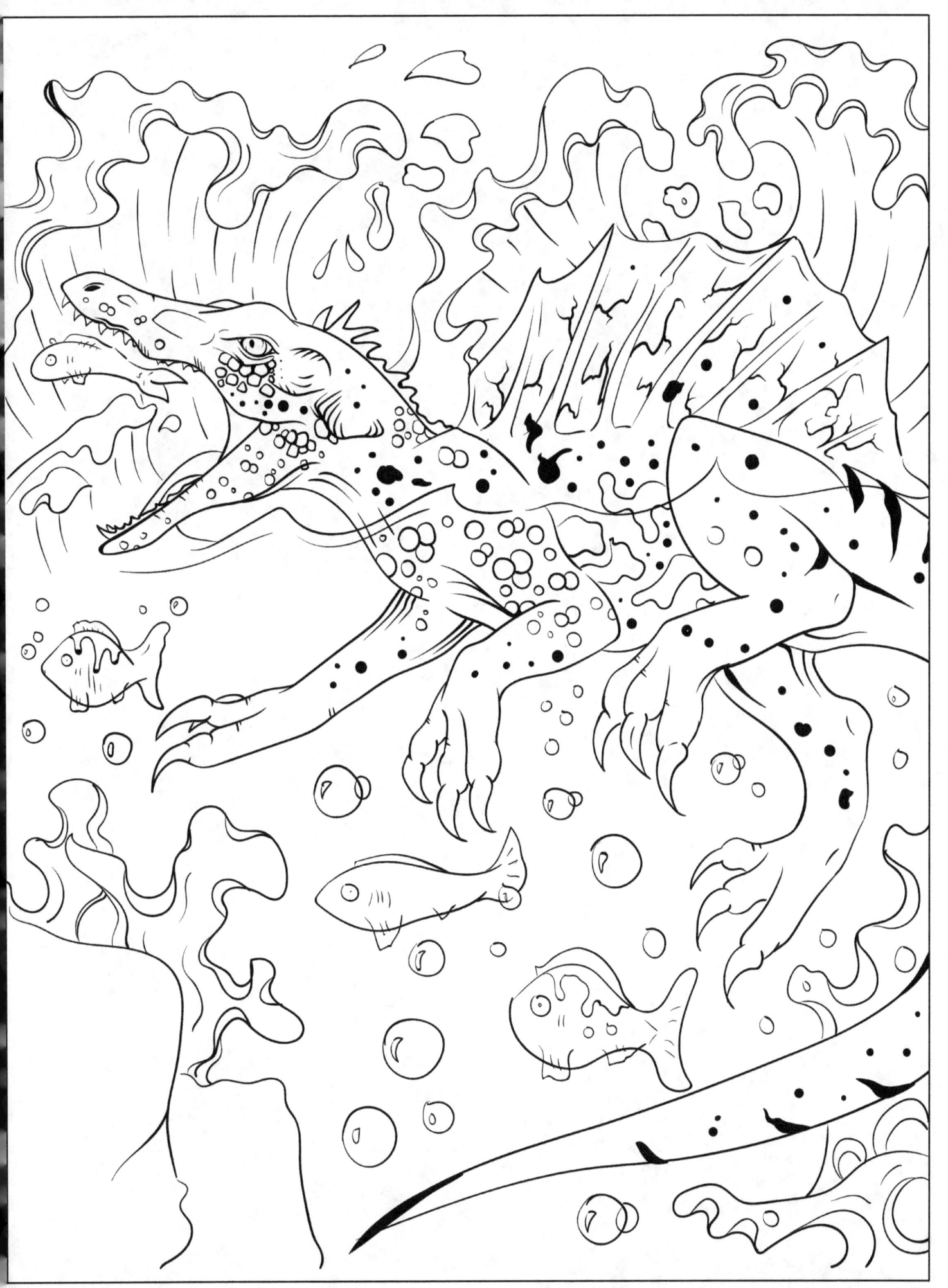

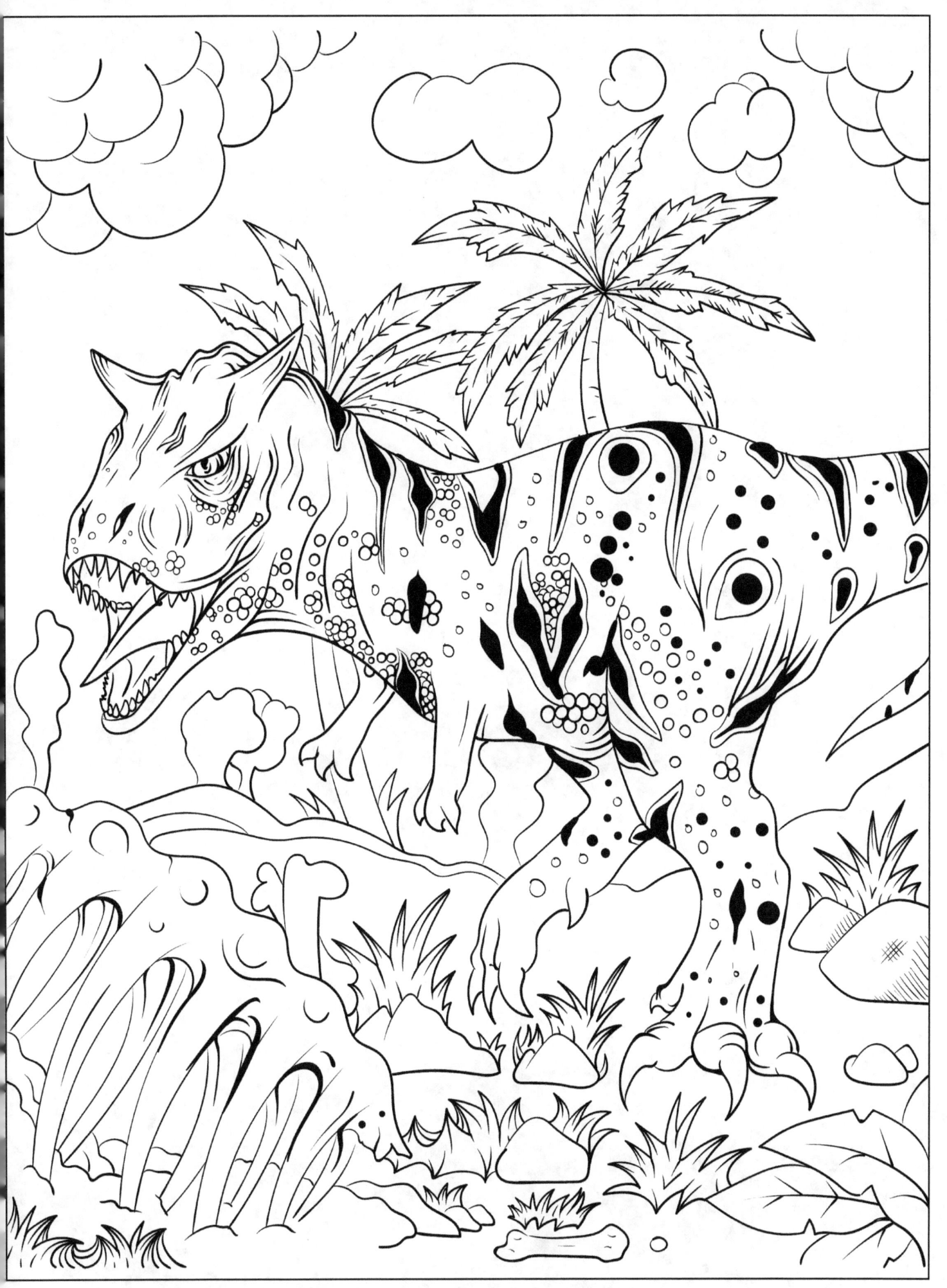

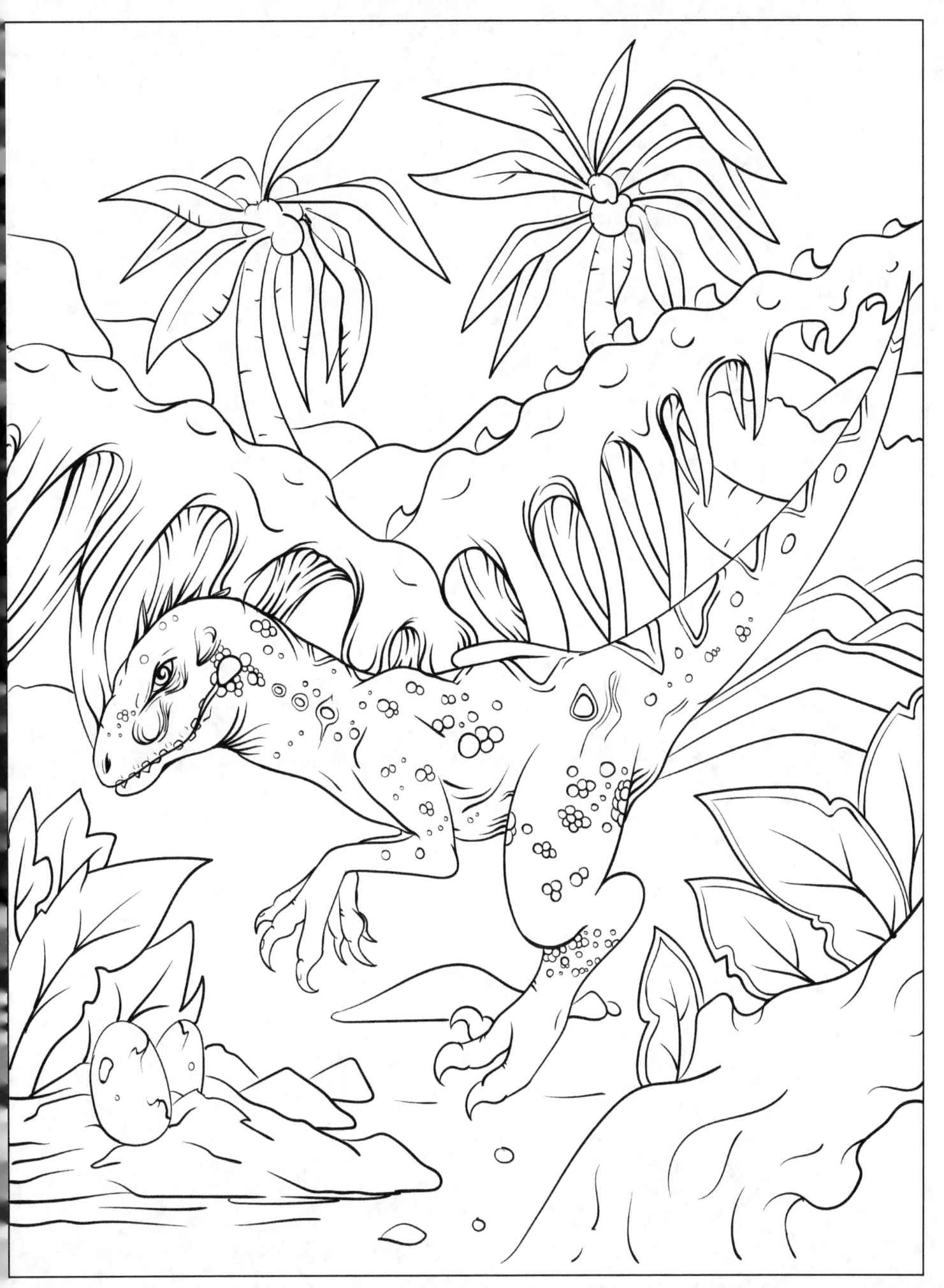

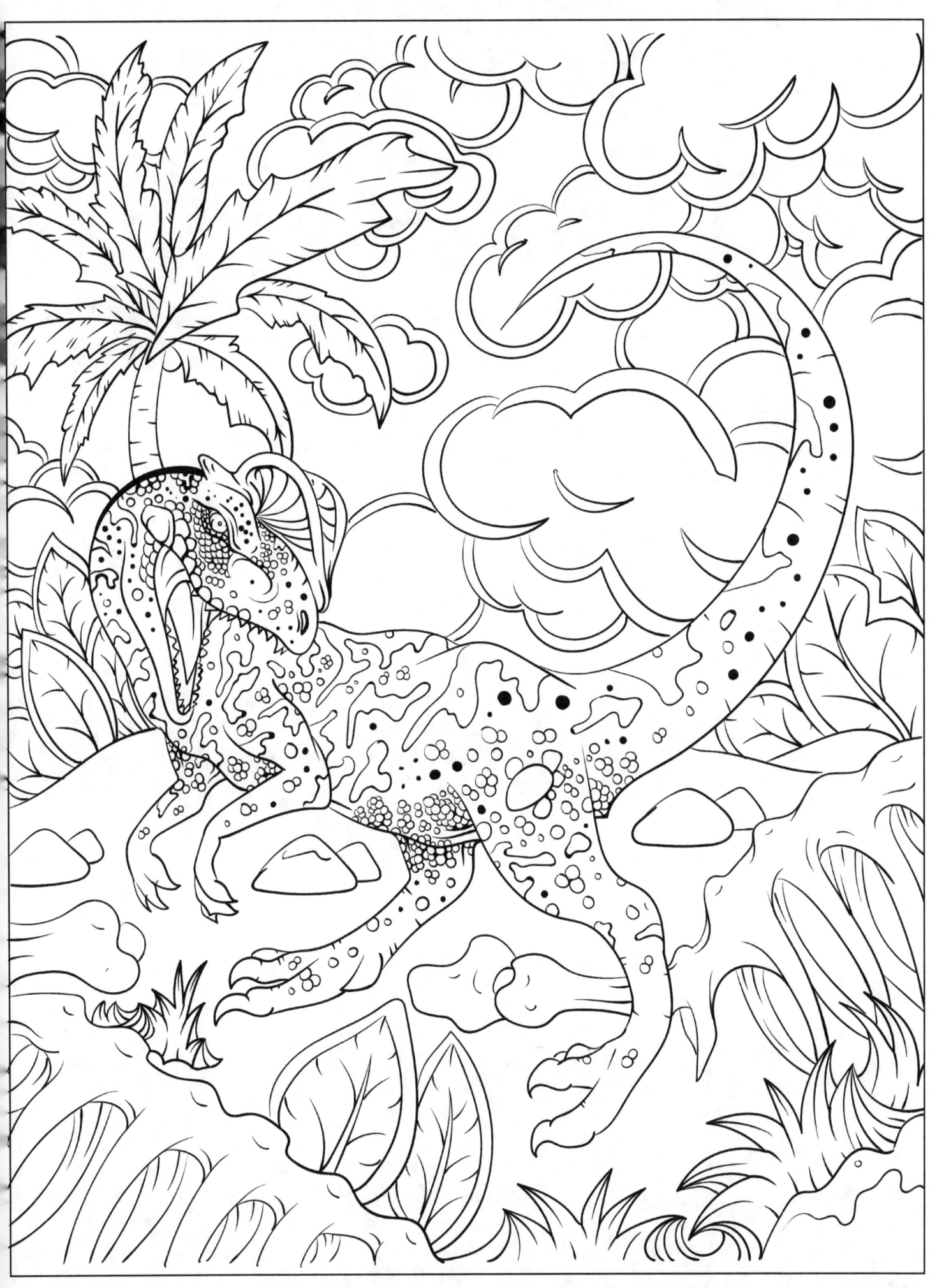

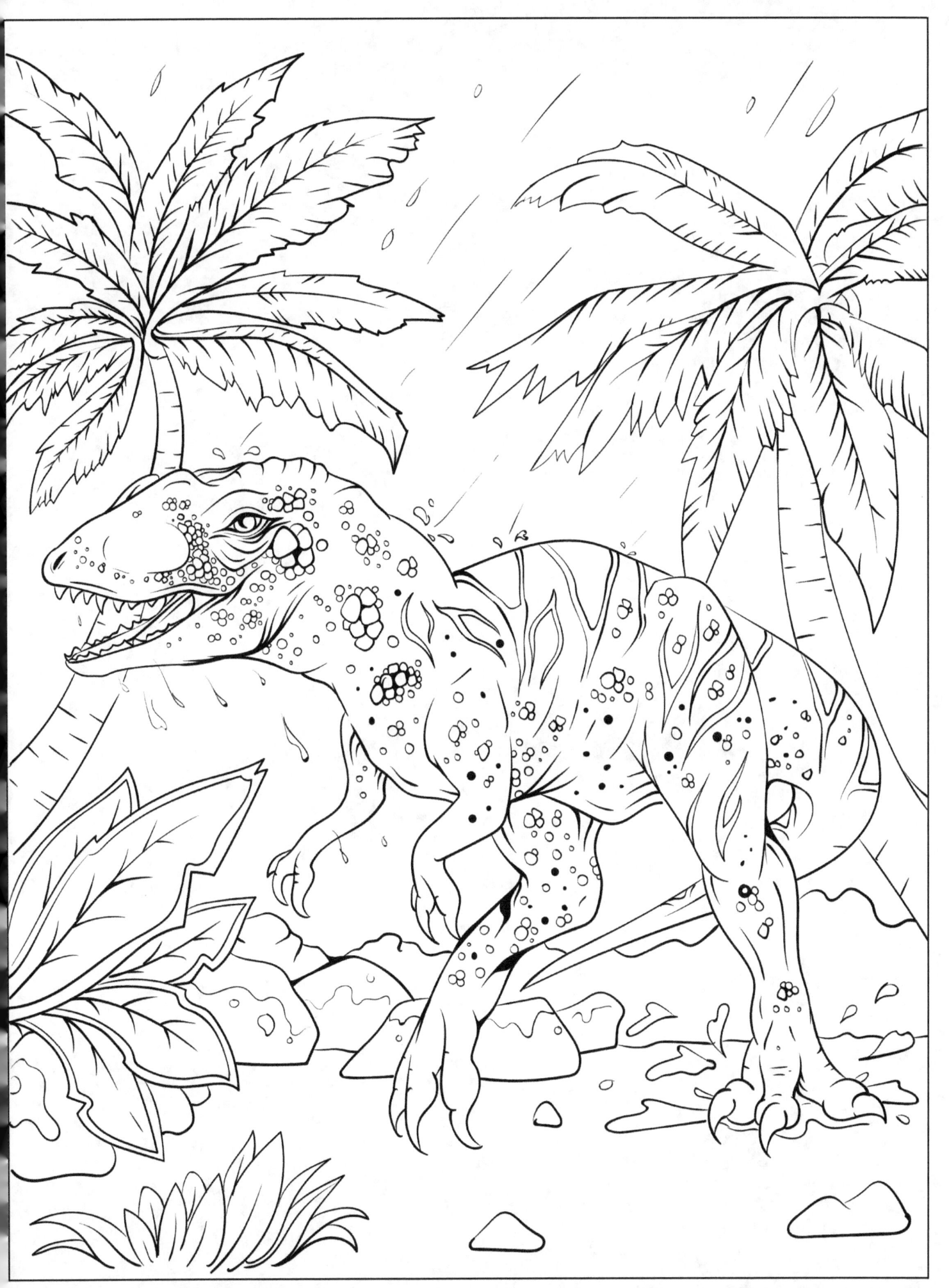

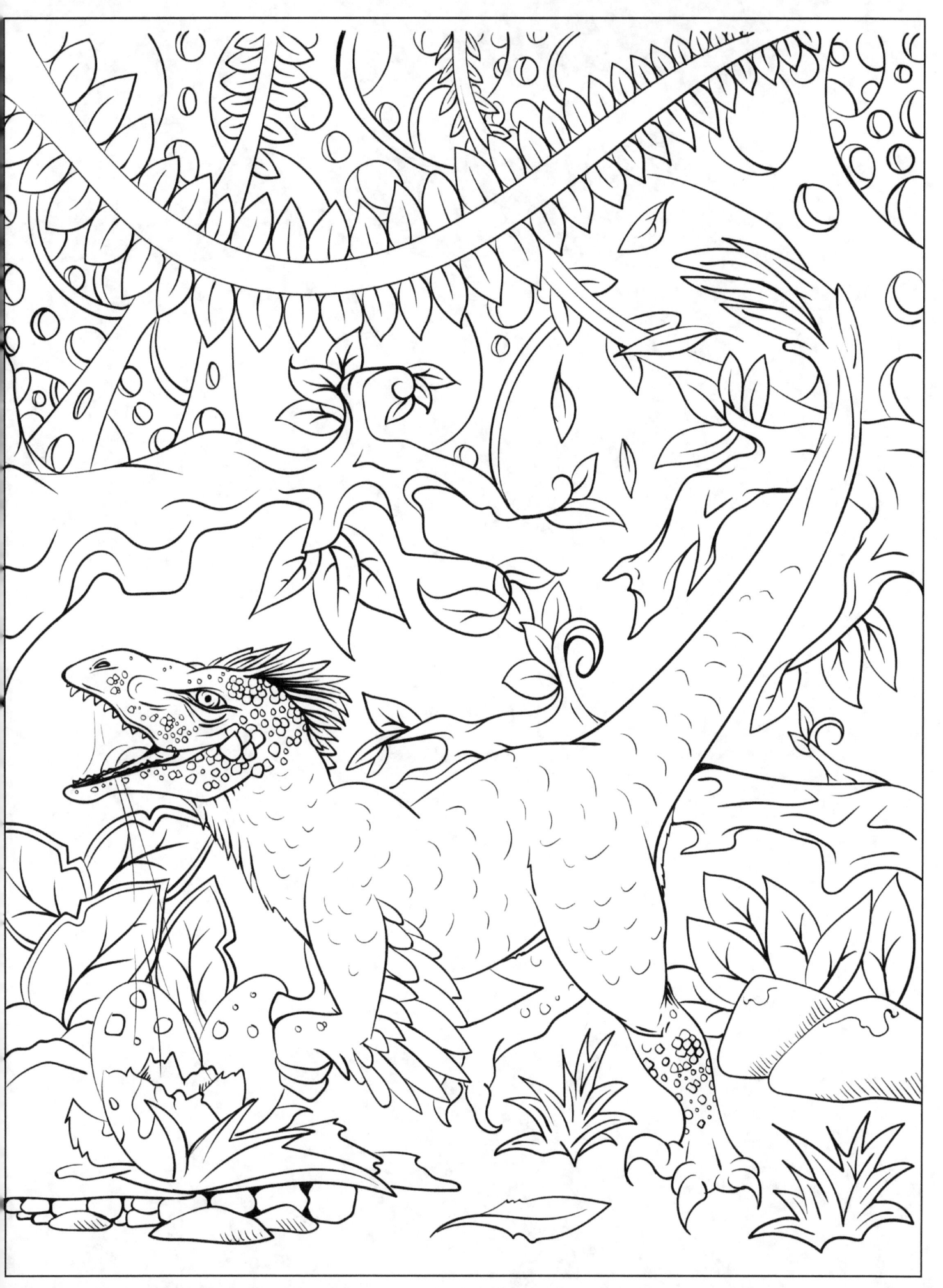

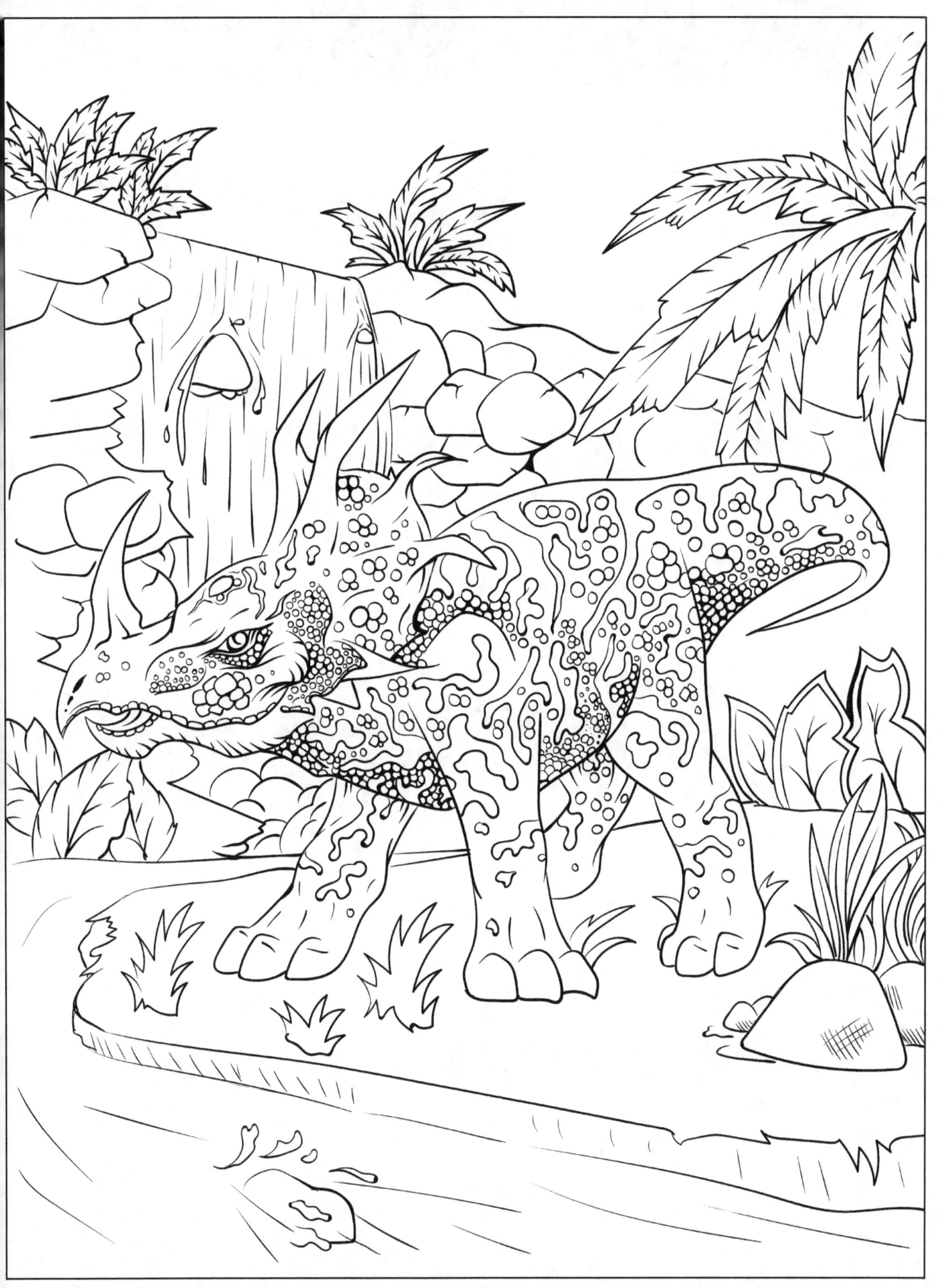

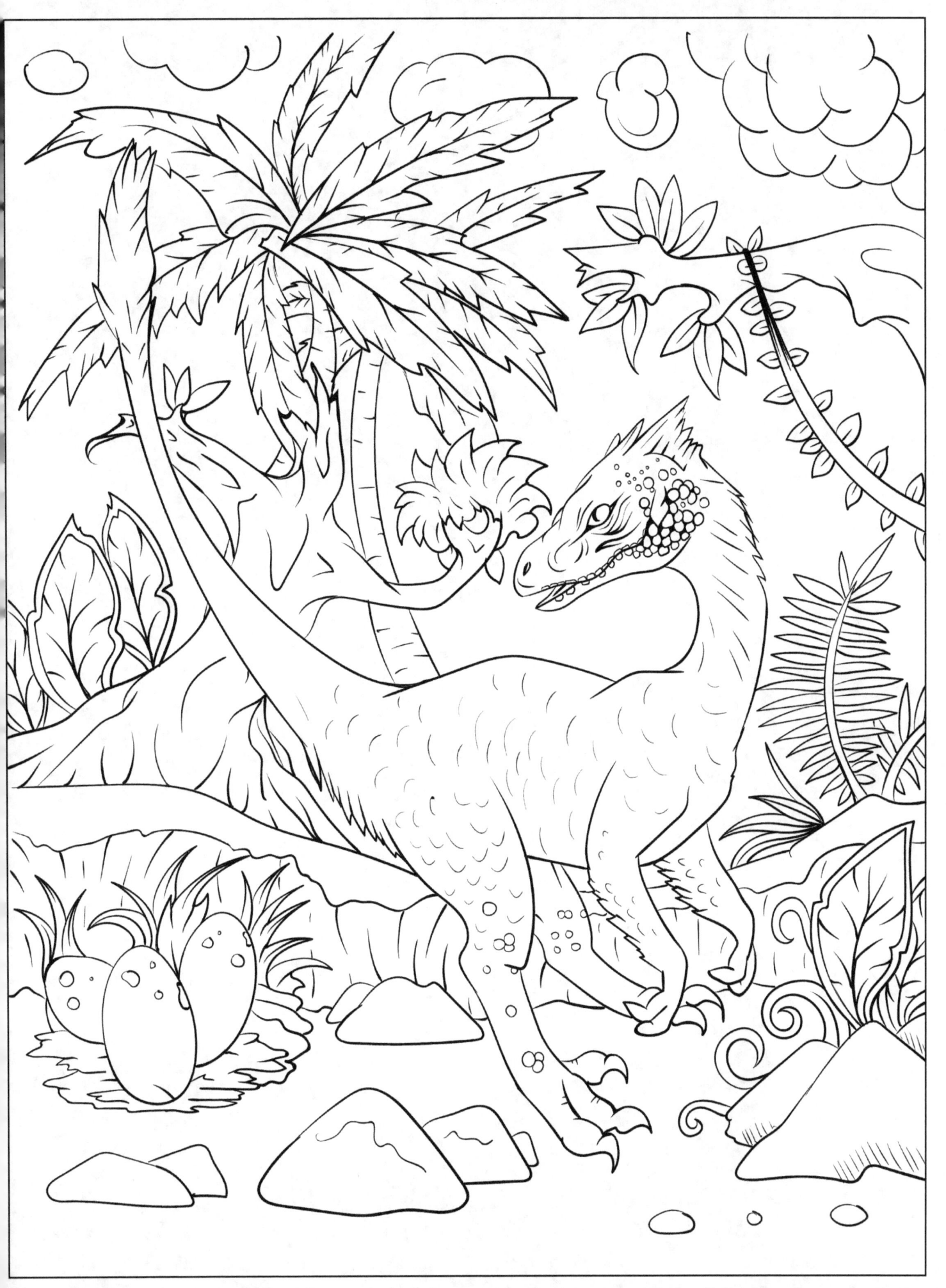

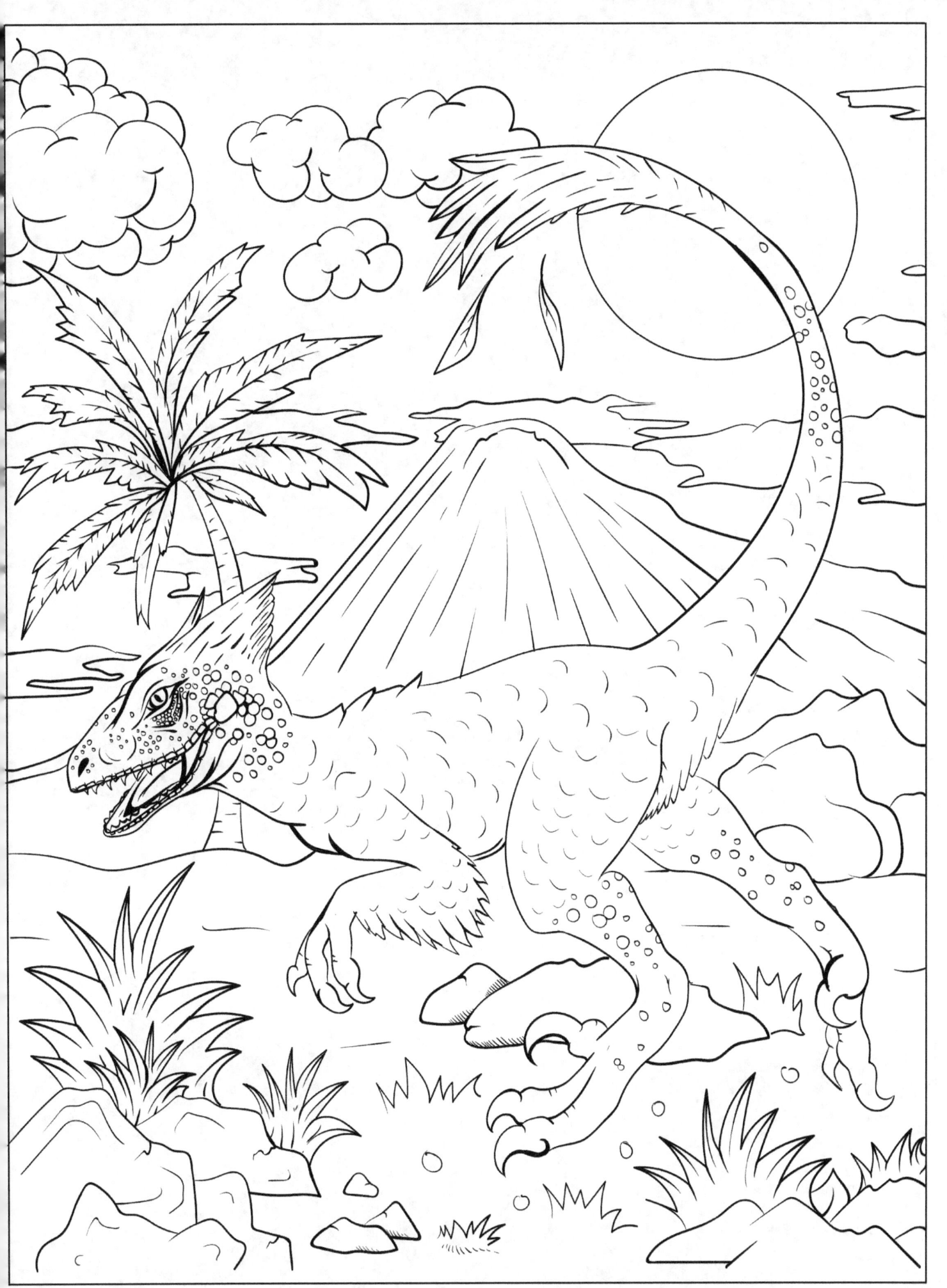

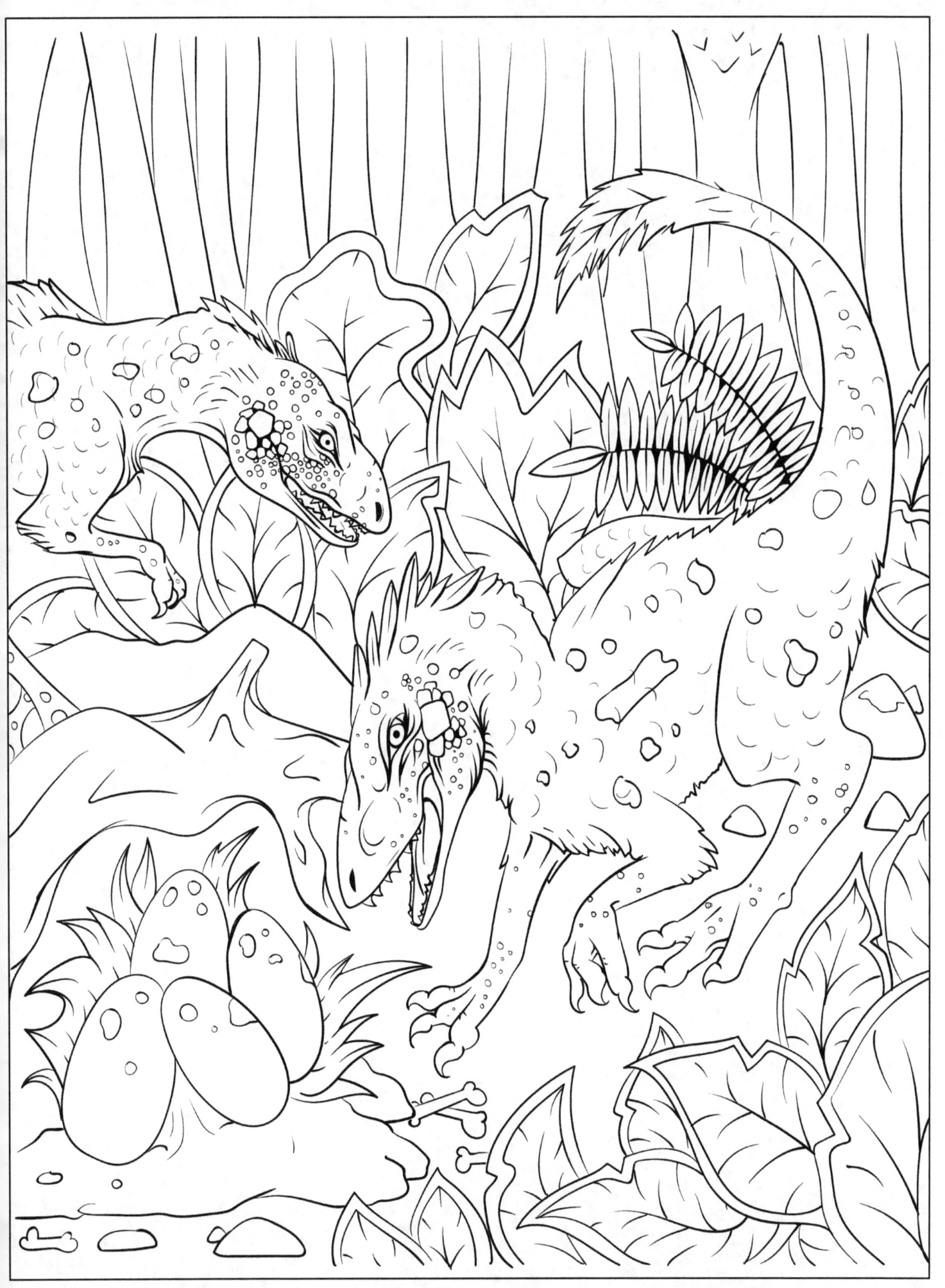

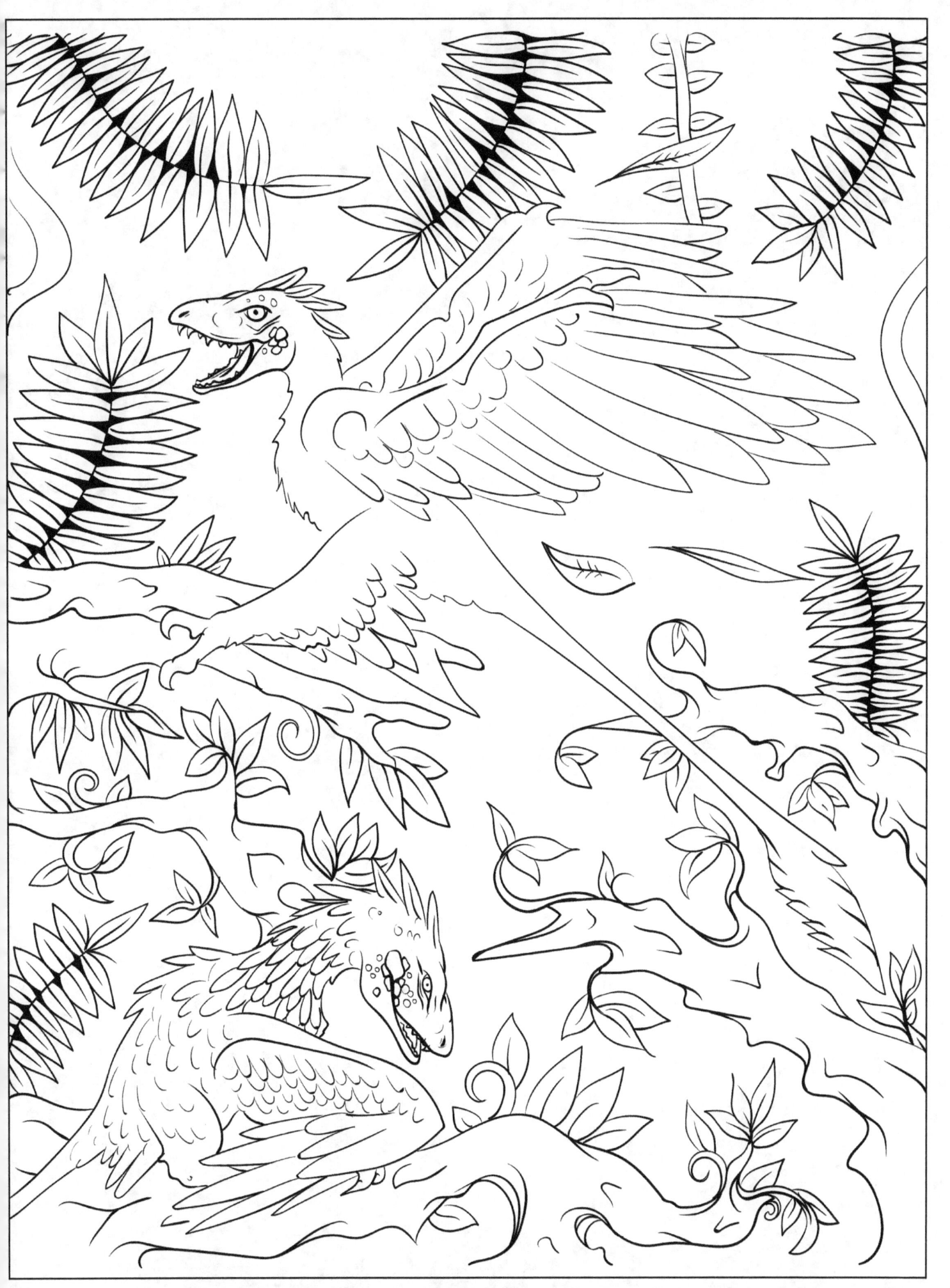

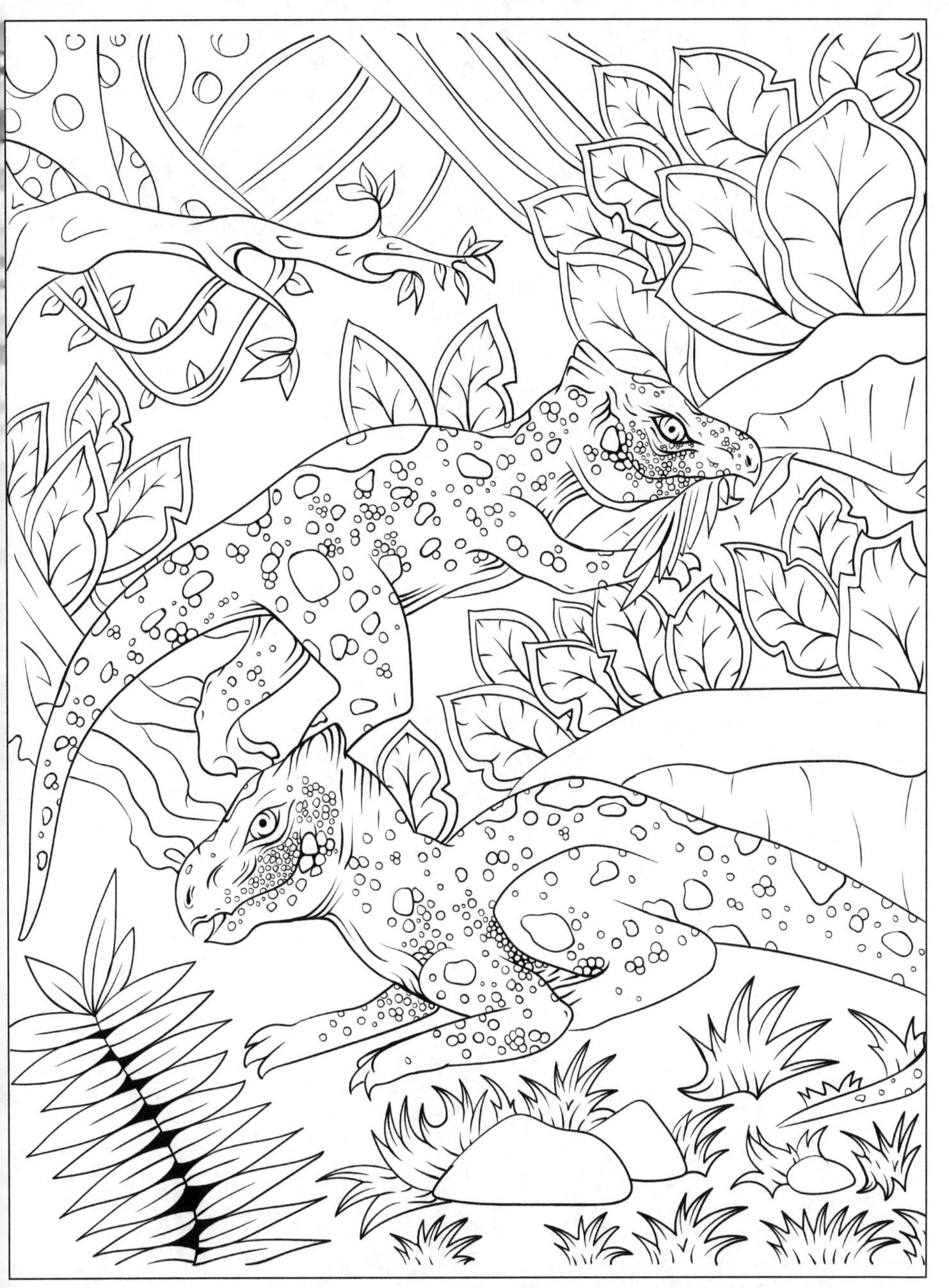

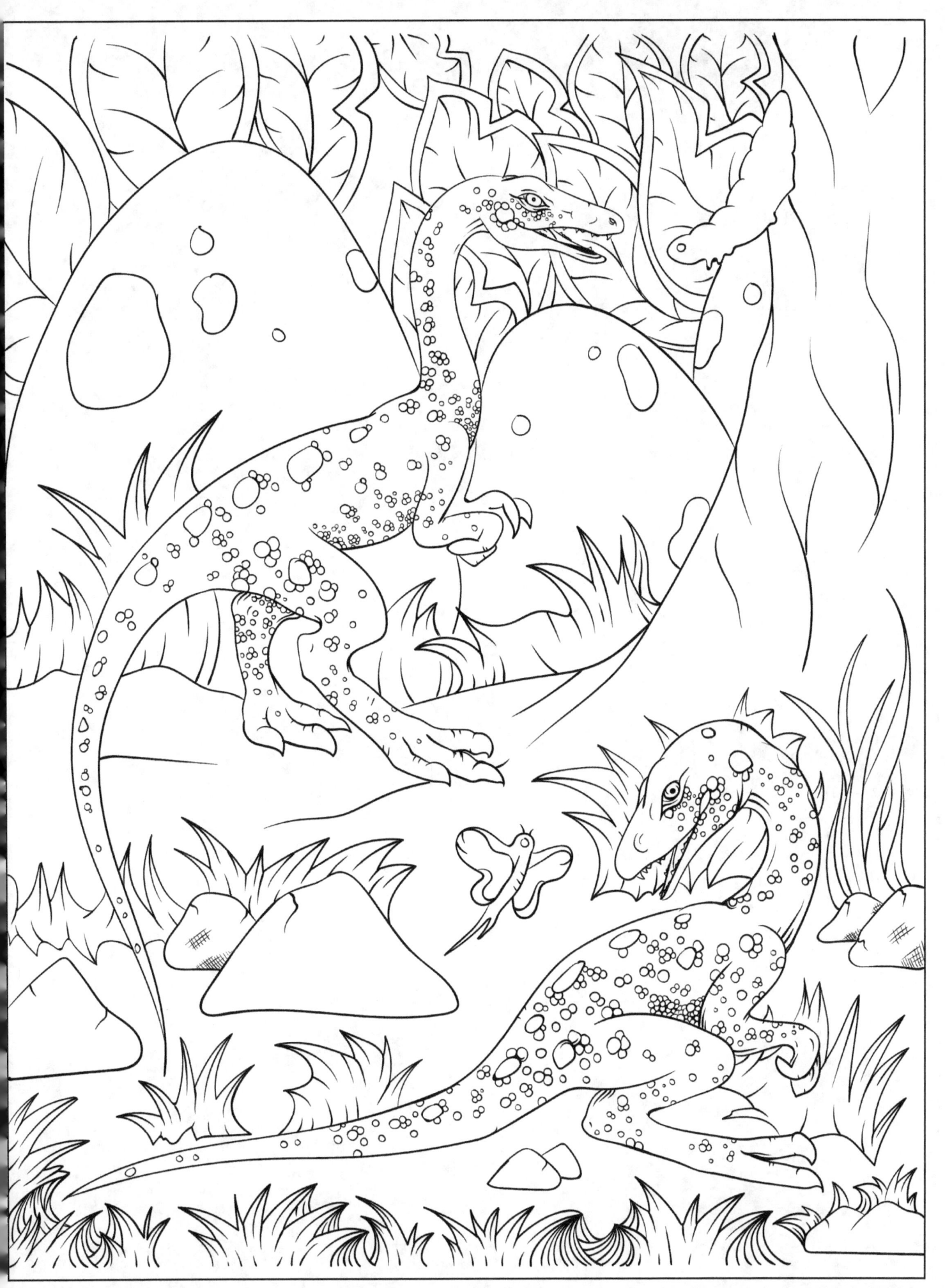

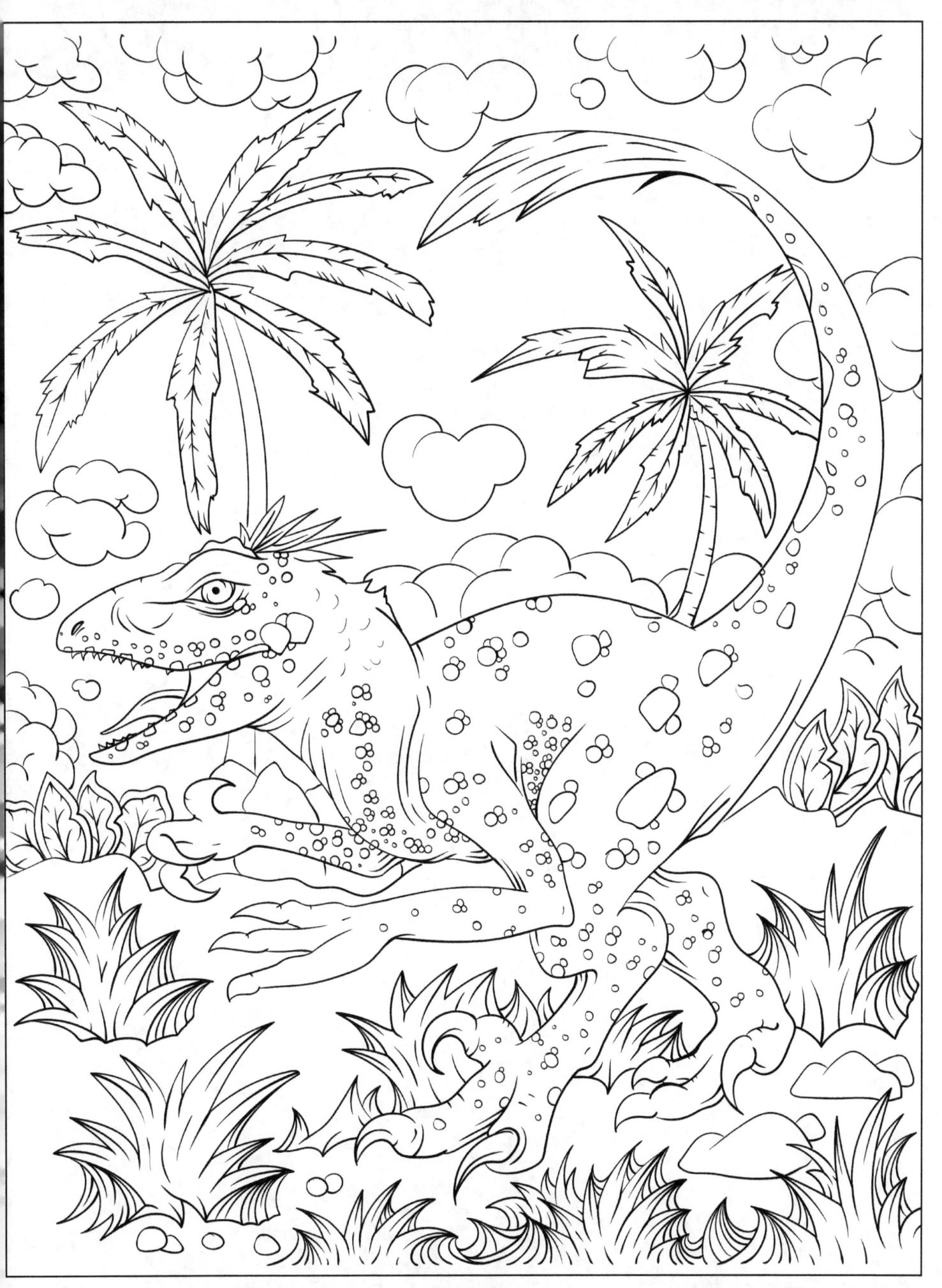

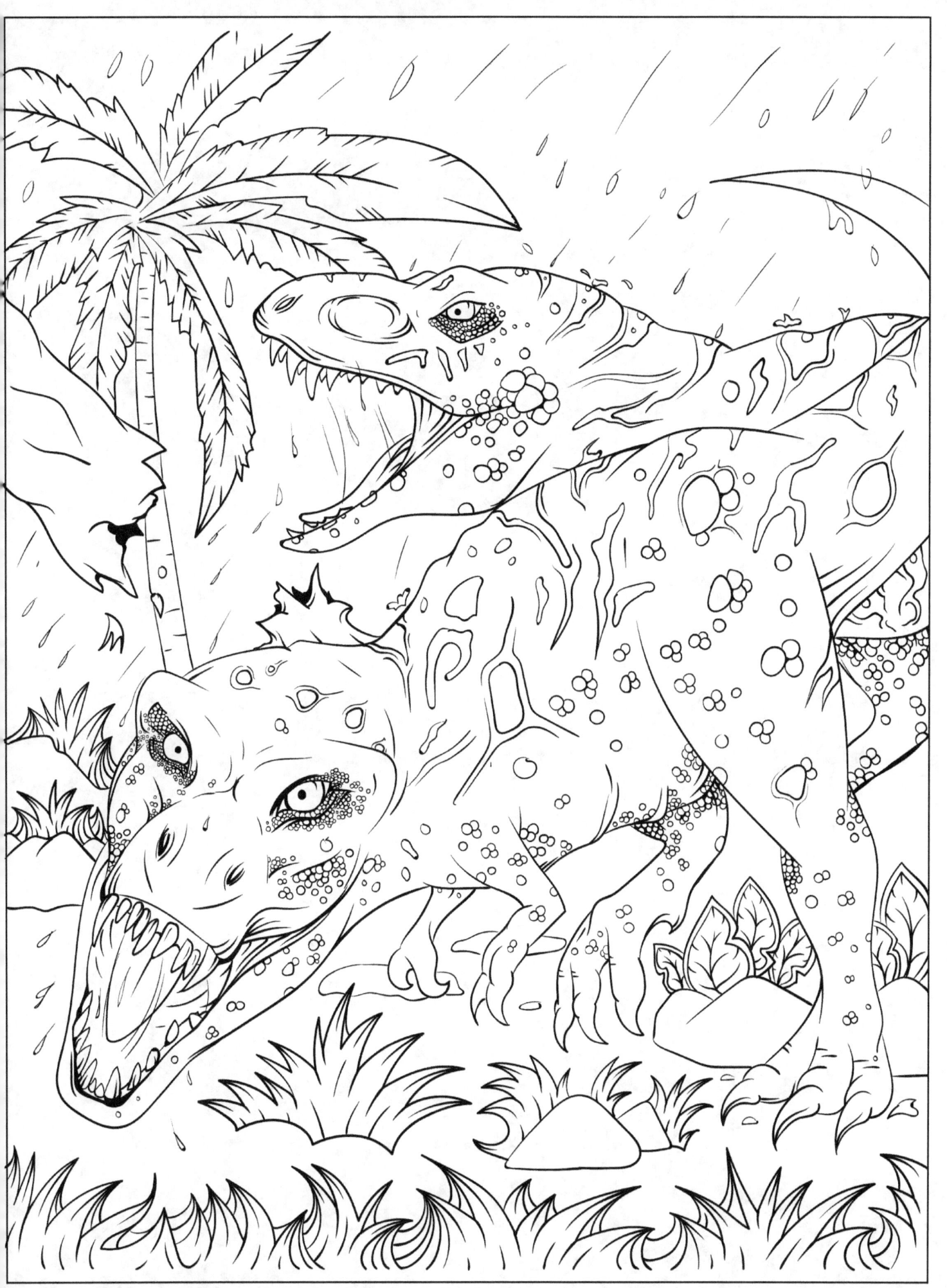

Featured Species used in this book:

Stegosaurus
Triceratops
Ankylosaurus
Apatosaurus
Brachiosaurus
Edmontosaurus
Parasauralophus
Corythosaurus
Dryosaurus
Gallimimus
Pachycephalosaurus
Tuojiangosaurus
Wuerhosaurus
Kritosaurus
Torosaurus
Plateosaurus
Amargasaurus
Deinocheirus
Rajasaurus
Tyrannotitan
Yutyrannus
Suchomimus
Ceratosaurus
Dimetrodon
Allosaurus
Spinosaurus
Carnotaurus
Deinonychus
Dilophosaurus
Giganotosaurus
Pyroraptor
Styracosaurus
Troodon
Velociraptor
Tanycolagreus
Microraptor
Archaeoceratops
Compsagnathus
Utahraptor
Tyrannosaurus Rex

ABOUT THE AUTHOR

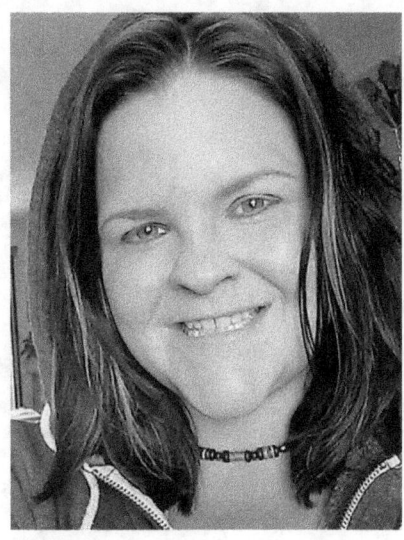

Kristy J Specht was born in Hastings, MN in 1983. She obtained her cosmetology license in 2009 and currently works as a hairstylist as of 2018. In March 2017 she earned her Associates in Graphic Design. The reason she created this book was because she has always been fascinated by dinosaurs from an early age. Her favorite movies include everything from the Jurassic Park series and also the newer Jurassic World series.

OTHER BOOKS:

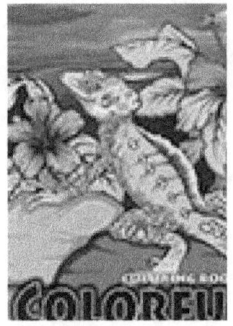

COLORFUL CRITTERS

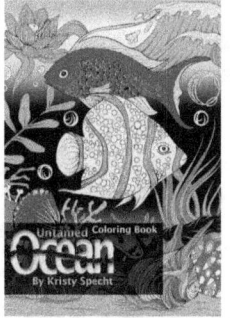

UNTAMED OCEAN

www.ingramcontent.com/pod-product-compliance
Lightning Source LLC
Chambersburg PA
CBHW080949170526
45158CB00008B/2421